a
Paris Year

MY DAY-TO-DAY ADVENTURES IN THE
MOST ROMANTIC CITY IN THE WORLD

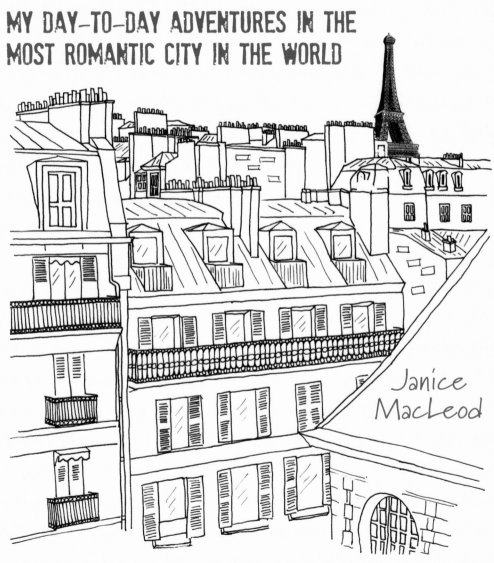

Janice
MacLeod

ST. MARTIN'S GRIFFIN   *New York*

www.stmartins.com

The Library of Congress Cataloging-in-Publication Data is available upon request.

ISBN 978-1-250-13012-9 (paper over board)
ISBN 978-1-250-13451-6 (e-book)

Our books may be purchased in bulk for promotional, educational, or business use. Please contact your local bookseller or the Macmillan Corporate and Premium Sales Department at 1-800-221-7945, extension 5442, or by e-mail at MacmillanSpecialMarkets@macmillan.com.

First Edition: June 2017

10 9 8 7 6 5 4 3 2 1

To Sharon Yamamoto,
who bought me the perfect coffee mug,
without which this book could not be made

"If I'm an advocate for anything, it's to move. As far as you can, as much as you can. Across the ocean, or simply across the river. The extent to which you can walk in someone else's shoes or at least eat their food, it's a plus for everybody. Open your mind, get up off the couch, move."

—Anthony Bourdain

Contents

Introduction

Paris is an old walking city. As you turn the corner of a medieval street and land on a bustling boulevard, you'll come across a plaque on a wall that states someone who did something great was either born, lived, or died in this apartment. Around another corner, you'll find another plaque with another fact. Or you'll take notice of the ornate lamps and discover they all have a consistent nautical theme, which will lead to days of searching for nautical themes around the city. You'll find them on park benches, schools, and statues.

As I made these little discoveries, I jotted them down in my travel journal. Eventually, these notes included a splash of paint, a few ink splatters from my temperamental fountain pen, and photos. I noticed patterns forming. Certain months had certain hues—pinks for spring, oranges for autumn, and delicate cool blues for winter. I also learned every day was named after a saint, so I began adding their names to the pages. Some days I would focus my camera on one shade of red, which looks alarmingly brilliant against the pale beige background of the architecture. Then I would try to replicate that red in my journal with my little set of watercolors. It was great fun. It still is. Paris is generous to the curious artist.

Often these sketches would lead to the creation of a Paris Letter. These are painted letters I create every month about life in Paris and send out snail-mail style to those who crave fun mail. It's refreshing to make something tangible in this electronic world.

This travel journal is a replication of my original notebooks. It is a memoir, a guidebook, and ode to ma belle Paris.

Allons-y! Let's go.

133, rue Mouffetard, 75005

1 Friday Vendredi

01

02

Bonjour

03

04 Life in Paris starts with a *Bonjour*. This is the magic word, the Open Sesame, that will turn you from an *étranger* (foreigner) to a local. It is to be said with confidence. No shy weak whispered greeting will do. It's best to be bellowed and followed with either Monsieur or Madame.

05

06

07 Once I pardonned and excusez-moied my way through the airport, I was ready to master the key word that would unlock my way into French life. I learned it by repeating the following two-phrase conversation daily with every familiar face:

08

09 "Bonjour Monsieur." (Hello sir.)

10 "Bonjour Madame." (Hello my lady.)
"Ça va?" (How are you?)

11 "Ça va." (I'm fine.) "Ça va?" (And you?)

12 "Ça va." (I'm fine, too.)
"Bonjour." (Have a good day.)

13 "Bonjour." (You, too.)

14 Bonjour Bonjour Ça va Ça va Ça va Ça va Bonjour Bonjour. It's really that easy to have an entire conversation in French.

15 There is no waving hello. This is not the French way. When you wave hello their eyes follow your hand like a litter of kittens. Non. They prefer words.

16

17

18

4 Monday Lundi

Week 1

01
02
03
04
05
06
07
08
09
10
11
12
13
14
15
16
17
18

Bonne Année et Bonne Santé

Happy New Year and wishes for good health are fluttering by on the breeze (Once the *Bonjour* is out of the way). Shopkeepers are slowly taking down the holiday decorations and are restocking for the year ahead. One of the loveliest of shopkeepers is Monsieur de Tugny.

For the last twenty-six years, he has owned Melodies Graphiques—a *papetière* a short stroll from the Seine on the Right Bank. He offers the most marvelous collection of pens, inks, and paper. When he's not seeing customers, he sits behind his desk and writes out wedding invitations. Our *monsieur* is also a professional calligrapher and lover of the written word . . . quite literally.

10, rue du Pont Louis-Philippe, 75004

5 Tuesday Mardi

01   I walked into his shop and told him I was in the market for
the best calligraphy pen. He leapt from his seat and scurried
02 around to the pen section. He sifted through a series of nibs and
in one eureka moment he chose one and attached it to a handle.
03 Beside the pens lay a massive book provided for pen testing. With
a flourish he flipped to a fresh page, dipped the pen in the ink
04 and wrote "Calligraphy." He turned to me. "The most beautifully
05 written word with the best pen. This is your pen." It wasn't the
most expensive pen, nor was it the most beautiful. I inquired about
06 those. He dismissed them with a wave and reminded me that
I had not asked for the most beautiful pen. I had asked for the
07 best. He returned to his desk to wrap my new pen. "I have the
08 best job in the world," he said. "The biggest problem someone has
in my *boutique* is to find the right pen, ink, and paper. These are
09 problems I can solve."

6 Wednesday Mercredi

01

02

03

04

05

06

07

09

"The wand chooses
the wizard, Mr. Potter."

—Mr. Ollivander in *Harry Potter and the Sorcerer's Stone,*
J. K. Rowling

7 Thursday Jeudi

Flea Market Finds

Week 1

I came upon a *brocante* today. These are mini flea markets that pop up around the city for a few days. You can tell a lot about a country based on the usual fare available at flea markets. With a very old country like France, you'll find vintage fashions, old dishes, and a surprising array of feathers. There is usually an old postcard stall, too, which is where I spend most of my time. I don't even bother looking at the front of postcards, thereby mystifying the seller. I'm after the lovely penmanship, stamp, and pastel patina of the postcard backs. After purchasing a stack, I zipped off to Angelina's café to further inspect my new acquisitions.

01
02
03
04
05
06
07
08
09
10
11
12
13
14
15
16
17
18

8 Friday Vendredi

01

02

03

04

05

06

07

08

09

10

Angelina's café serves the world's finest hot chocolate. It's a thick
11 brew that surely sticks to the ribs. Usually I order up a cup to go at
the front cashier. It's the same hot chocolate as in the tearoom but
12 half the price. Today though, I've got vintage postcards to peruse and
my own postcards to write with my new fountain pen, so I've taken
13 a seat in the back corner of the tearoom to watch the old gents
and dames on display. They often sit alone, dressed up.
14 The men in suits. The ladies draped in jewels, slowly
sipping their hot chocolates. Demure peacocks.

16

17

18

226, rue de Rivoli, 75001

ST. PAULIN DAY

11 Monday Lundi

He was doing mathematics.
With a fountain pen.

Week 2

01

02

03

04

05

06

07

08

09

10

11

12

13

14

15

16

17

18

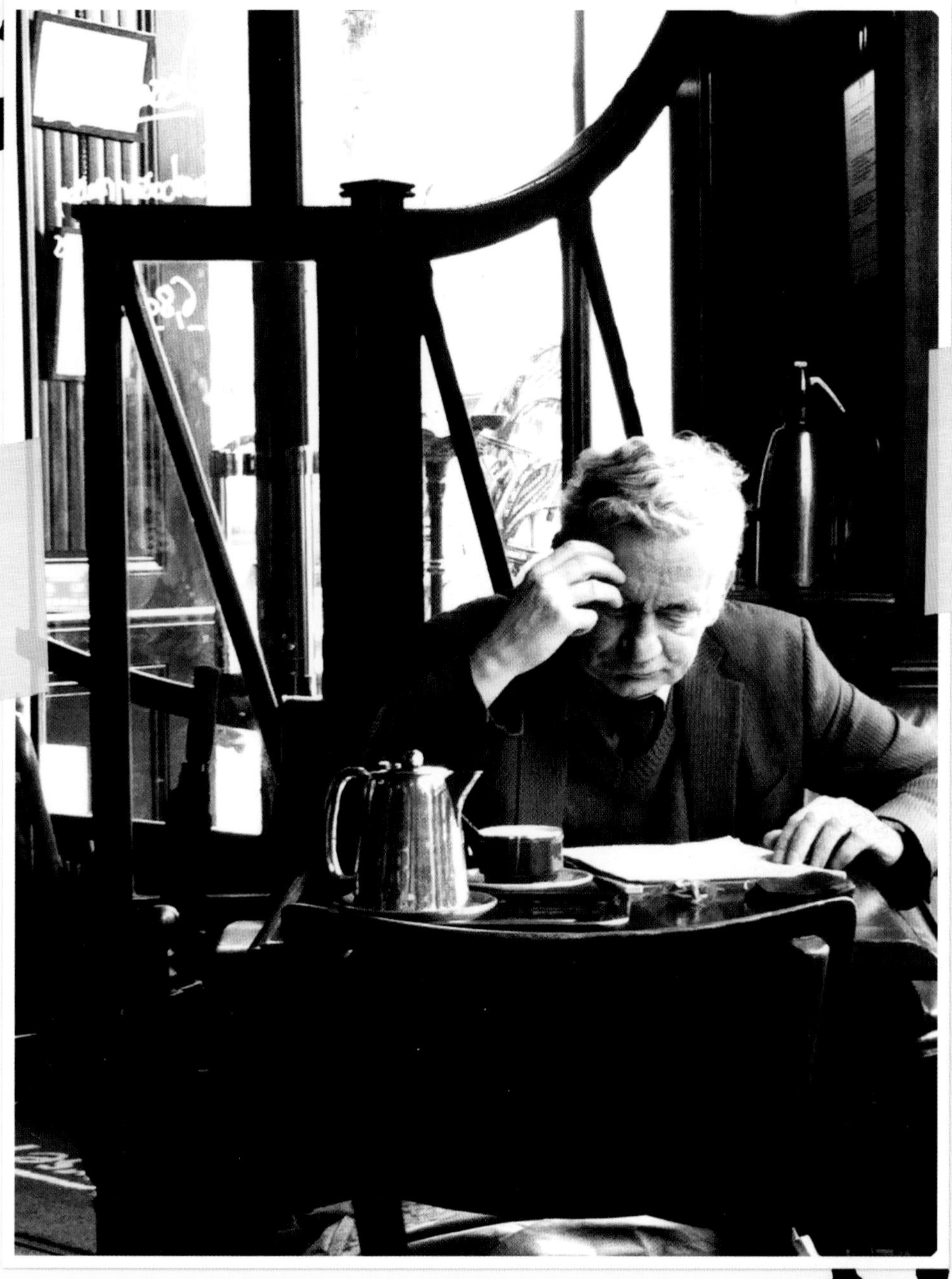

12 Tuesday Mardi

Week 2

The Routine

We all our have our daily routines. When you've lived in Paris for some time, you develop an affinity for *boutiques* that stem out of a thirty-minute walk from your front door. Paris is, after all, a walking city and having a destination gives purpose to your walk—a "somewhere to be" hustle. One of my preferred destinations is a newspaper store in the 6th *quartier*. Browsing the stacks of magazines I pretend to read, I watch the same cast of characters come and go—a bellowing *"Bonjour,"* a few coins offered, a newspaper tucked under the arm and an *"Au revoir"* until tomorrow. Do they notice me, too? If so, do they also find the daily intersecting of our lives charming? Unlikely. I imagine they continue on with another destination in mind. *C'est la vie à Paris.*

4, rue Grégoire de Tours, 75006

ST. YVETTE DAY

13 Wednesday Mercredi   *Week 2*

01

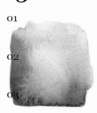

02

03

04

05

06

07

08

09

10

11

12

13   Hemingway had watering holes thirty minutes in each direction
      from his front door. He lived here after the war, when a slew
14   of American expats flocked to Paris to live on the cheap. You
      can't say it's cheap these days, but it is still worth it.

15   "Paris was always worth it and you received return for
16   whatever you brought to it. But this is how Paris was in the
      early days when we were very poor and very happy."
17   —Hemingway, *A Moveable Feast*

18

Haunted by Hemingway

There is no doubt that Hemingway is here in Paris. In death, he relives every moment of his life when he lived here back when he was just Ernest. After reading his book, *A Moveable Feast*, a memoir of his time in Paris, quotes from the book permeated my days. At bars, when Christophe would go outside to shake a familiar hand, the invisible Hemingway would whisper in my ear. So clear. Haunting sparse words, lines from the book, and encouragements just for me. All literary problems were solved in those two-minute breaks. When Christophe would return, I could feel Hemingway turn away and return to his whiskey. He was my ghost and mine alone. On long walks, Hemingway walked beside me, pointing out something to be sure I didn't miss detailed carvings in a doorway, a new piece of graffiti on a wall, a book I should read. All those little details made their way into my notes. He was a benevolent companion, guiding me toward my own memoir of Paris.

"You belong to me and all Paris belongs to me and I belong to this notebook and this pencil."

—Hemingway, *A Moveable Feast*

15 Friday Vendredi   *Week 2*

01

The Polidor

02

03 Being haunted by Hemingway includes haunting his haunts. And one
of the more notable is the Polidor restaurant for its famed *boeuf*
04 *bourguignon.* I found I was reaching for the saltshaker a little too
often with this fanciful beef stew. Is this one of those restaurants
05 famous for being famous? And after time no one remembers why it
was famous in the first place?

06

Was it once the only show in town and that's why it was
07 famous? If so, it's hardly the only show in town now. It's surrounded
by restaurants that add, dare I say it, salt. But the ambiance is
08 nice and the house wine is cheap and fair, and maybe that's enough
09 to make it famous.

10

11

18

41, rue Monsieur le Prince, 75006

18 Monday Lundi   *Week 3*

01

Scott
& Zelda

02

03

04

05

06

07

08

09

10

11 When haunted by Hemingway, one can't help but have F. Scott and
    Zelda Fitzgerald along for the ride. They lived in Paris at the
12 same time as other American writers were flocking to the city
    during the 1920s. Scott met Zelda when he was a soldier. She
13 wouldn't marry him because he couldn't support them on his meager
    writer's salary. Eventually he signed a book deal and she accepted
14 his proposal. You can see how *The Great Gatsby* story line came
    along when you look at the true history of the Fitzgeralds.
15 Eventually, Zelda lost her mind and was admitted to a psychiatric
    hospital where she later died. But when they were in Paris, life
16 was a circus and they were the stars of the show.
17

18
                                                    16, rue du Parc Royal, 75003

19 Tuesday Mardi   *Week 3*

01 "I don't suppose I really know you very well—but I know you smell
like the delicious damp grass that grows near old walls and that your
02 hands are beautiful opening out of your sleeves and that the back of
your head is a mossy sheltered cave when there is trouble in the
03 wind and that my cheek just fits the depression in your shoulder."
04   —Zelda Fitzgerald

05

06

07

08

09

10

11

12

13 "He told me how he had first met her during the war and then
lost her and won her back. . . . This first version that he told me
14 of Zelda and a French naval aviator falling in love was a truly sad
story and I believe it was a true story. Later he told me other
15 versions of it as though trying them for use in a novel, but none was
as sad as this first one and I always believed the first one. . . . They
16 were better told each time; but they never hurt you the same
way the first one did."
17   —Hemingway, *A Moveable Feast*

18

01

Captive on the Carousel of Time

02

03

04

05

0(

0'

0{

09

10

11

12 Grief can be so dramatic at times. Each year, Paris plops extra
carousels around the city for the holiday season. A gift from the
13 mayor to citizens and visitors of Paris. Today they started hauling
14 the carousels back on the trucks. A kid stood screaming his head
off. He screamed with such passion that even our local homeless
15 guy, The Spaniard, stopped fighting with his invisible friend to watch
the meltdown. The parents stood by, waiting it out, while the sullen
16 carousel worker loaded the horses into the truck, visibly distressed
17 over the toddler's fiasco.

18

21 Thursday Jeudi

01 02
Speaking of Screaming One's Head Off...

03 France's King Louis XVI was beheaded in Paris
04 on this date in 1793. He inherited a mess from
the lavish spending of predecessors. Some French
05 kings were revered, even worshipped, but this
Louis was considered a joke.
06

07 Unemployment in Paris was about 50 percent,
crops were failing and food prices were high.
08 This is where foraging came into play. *Escargots—*
snails—were a war food. Protein, free for the
09 picking, from the forest floor.

10 On the morning of January 21, Louis was
dressed by his valet and brought in a green
11 carriage to the courtyard of what is now place
de la Concorde. The king stepped out of the
12 carriage, removed his outer garments, folded
them neatly, then offered his hands to be bound
13 by a handkerchief. The execution was hastily
carried out. A lone cry of *"Vive la République!"*
14 was heard, and soon the crowds cheered the
death of the king.
15

16 Now, when the city paints a park bench
and booksellers paint bookstalls along the Seine,
17 they all must paint with the same shade, called
18 Carriage Green.

01
Carriage Green
02

16

25 Monday Lundi *Week 4*

01
Wallace Fountains

02 The Wallace fountains are found throughout Paris. They are
03 painted Carriage Green and were brought here by philanthropist
Richard Wallace. He thought it a travesty that the great walking
04 city of Paris didn't offer free drinking water to quench the
thirst of walkers, so he created a fountain featuring four lovely
05 sisters—kindness, simplicity, charity, and sobriety. The water
06 flows behind their arms so you just have to reach in with your
water bottle for a free fill. This water is still the main source
07 of drinking water for the homeless. How kind, simple, charitable,
and, well, sober-maintaining. My preferred fountain is outside my
08 preferred bookstore. Book browsing makes me thirsty.

09
10
11
12
13
14
15
16
17
18

37, rue de la Bûcherie, 75005

19

01

02

03

04

05

06

07

There is nothing special about Paris in January, and that's exactly what makes it so. Too early for tourists, mayhem from the holidays is a memory, and Christmas trees have been tossed in a pile in the park to await the city's army of trucks to haul them away. Each tiny apartment feels like Versailles now that the guests are gone and the decorations have been stored. All that remains is the city's twinkle lights, bejeweling streets and boulevards, but even those slowly disappear, taken down string by string by men with tall ladders.

08

09

10

11

12

13

14

15

16

17

18

27 Wednesday Mercredi   *Week 4*

01

Shakespeare & Company

02 English speakers and readers flock to Shakespeare & Co. on
03 the Left Bank of the Seine in the heart of the Latin Quarter
to gobble up copies of *A Moveable Feast* by our ghostly Ernest
04 Hemingway. The store is stocked with new editions, plus old
copies donated along the way. After the 2015 Paris attacks,
05 the world went into a depletion for the book. No one could find
it anywhere. Unless, of course, you knew where to look.
06

07 The original owner was Sylvia Beach and the shop was at
12, rue de l'Odéon. George Whitman opened the current shop.
08 His daughter runs it now. She is
named after Sylvia.

09

10

11

12

13

14

15

16

17

18

When Hemingway wrote of Sylvia, he says she was kind, that she had a lively face, and that she loved to make jokes and gossip.

"No one that I ever knew was nicer to me."

—Hemingway, *A Moveable Feast*

RAINER MARIA RILKE WROTE ABOUT THE SHOPS OF THE LATIN QUARTER WITH THEIR SHOP WINDOWS FILLED WITH OLD BOOKS AND ETCHINGS WHERE NOBODY SEEMED TO ENTER AND THE PROPRIETOR COULD BE SEEN READING PEACEFULLY INDIFFERENT TO WORLDLY SUCCESS. BESIDE HIM LIES A DOG OR PERHAPS A CAT.

SHAKESPEARE AND CO

WHILE THY BOOK LIVE AND WE HAVE WITS TO READ

THOU ART ALIVE STILL

AND PRAISE TO GIVE

RARE BOOKS FIRST EDITIONS

29 Friday Vendredi

01
Les "Pas Possibles"

02 The French are the most wonderful people on the planet, except
03 for those who work at the visa office. They are pure evil.
Legally living in Paris is frustrating and time-consuming. Everything
04 is always "pas possibles," not possible, with these visa office
administrators, even though it may have been entirely possible
05 before. I accept their antics with a dopey grin, nod that I mostly
understand, and silently curse that I don't have the language
06 skills to argue. I even pray to Saint Gildas, who you pray to for
07 deliverance from evil. Pure evil. After my interview with the
devil incarnate, I left defeated with an extension and another
08 appointment in three months to do this again. But there was a
glimmer of hope on the way home. Encouraging graffiti, perhaps a
09 message from a saint: All is possible.

10

11

12

13

14

15

16

17

18

1 Monday Lundi

01   But it wasn't all bad at the visa office. I sat next to an Italian man. He had his bike helmet and a thick *dossier* of paperwork on

02 his lap. Two hours in, he noticed there were no people being called into the office. Nostrils flared, he stood up and walked right in like

03 a boss. He discovered that the entire office had left for their long lunches. The place was deserted. Incensed, he walked out to the

04 waiting room and announced the news. He began ranting in the most beautiful French I have ever heard. French with an Italian accent is

05 a symphony of rolling Rs and spitty Ps. When he was done his rant,

06 I wanted to applaud. He stormed out and, I believe, hopped on his

07 motorcycle and drove back to Italy.

08

ST.THÉOPHANE DAY

2 Tuesday Mardi

01

La vie est faite de petits bonheurs.

02

(Life is full of small pleasures.)

03

04

05

06

07

08

09

10

11

12

13

14

15

16

17

18

3 Wednesday Mercredi   *Week 5*

01
With all the museums in Paris, it's easy to be inspired by old artists,
02 but modern artists are just as inspiring, like the graffiti artists who
give us whimsical, thought-provoking art at every turn. One modern
03 artist who inspires me is American photographer Nichole Robertson.
She decided one day to walk out of her Paris apartment and take
04 photos of one color. One day it was yellow, another day blue. Inspired,
05 I took a few days to study red.

06

07

08

09

10

11

12

13

14

15

16

17

18

4 Thursday Jeudi

01

02 Is it the creamy neutral palette of the buildings and gray skies that make red pop?

03

04 Robertson published a book called *Paris in Color*, where she took photos of Paris and

05 organized them by color. She

06 followed it with another book, *Paris in Love*. This time the

07 entire book was photos of red found around Paris.

08

09 Once I made my way through red, I'd follow with

10 other colors. Eventually, I would pick a theme and shoot that for

11 a day: statues, neon, textures, and such. It was great fun and

12 this study of a certain subject sharpens the eye. Plus, it makes

13 a stroll even more satisfying. It's

14 like an Easter egg hunt.

15

16

17

18

ST. AGATHE DAY

5 Friday Vendredi

01

02

03

"Red demands your attention. Red draws you in. Whether it's a towering Métro sign, a bold door, or a tiny tangle of flowers in a window box that lures you from the end of a long street, when Paris wears red, she seduces."

—Nichole Robertson, *Paris in Love*

04

05

06

07

08

09

10

11

12

13

14

15

16

17

18

8 Monday Lundi

01

Lady Métro

02

03

04

05

06

07

08

09

10

11

12

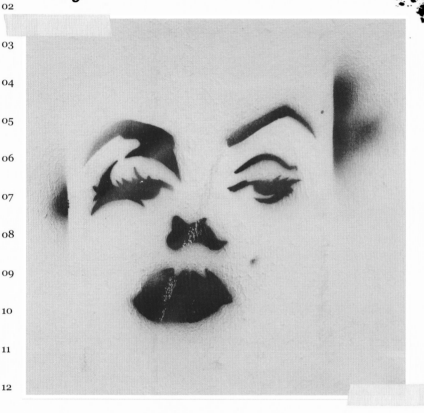

13

For a time I met Lady Métro on the platform where her Métro
14 line and mine intersected. She was 30 years my senior, which to
me excused the napping mid-conversation. She was lulled by the
15 soft rumble of the train that would take us to a new tea shop or
award-winning *boulangerie*. On the stop before ours, I would say,
16 "So . . .," which would startle her awake and she would immediately
17 start talking, pretending she hadn't drifted off.

18

01   She carried spoons in her purse. Plastic spoons she lifted

02   along the way. Picard, the frozen food store, seemed to always be on our path, or was it her path? It was hard to tell. Her

03   plans seemed so innocent, yet I always sensed I was about to get hoodwinked, like when we went to Picard she would "notice"

04   the cherry pistachio ice cream. A two-pack. Back on the street she'd hand me her extra spoon. "If I buy two, I eat two." Mild,

05   but still hoodwinked. I ate it even though I didn't like cherry

06   pistachio. She offended easily.

07

08

09

10

11

12

13

14

15

16

17

18

10 Wednesday Mercredi   *Week 6*

01
    I didn't introduce her to my friends. There were hints but I
shrugged them off and never followed through. I didn't trust her.
02
She spoke poorly of others. I knew she would eventually speak
poorly of me once I was no longer novel, or once she had harvested
03
all she could from me, or once her needs were met.

04
    Plus, she seemed to take up the whole room. You just can't
introduce an elephant to a herd of sheep and expect the relationship
05
to flourish.

06

07

08

09

10

11

12

13

14

15

16

17

18

11 Thursday Jeudi   *Week 6*

01   When she caught on, her hints turned to allegations. She
wanted me to toss the baton. Find someone else who could wake
02   her when it was time to go. So, it turns out, once I could not
fulfill her future needs and it was clear that I wouldn't toss
03   that baton, I was pushed to the margins of her daily life and
eventually off the calendar altogether. It lasted eleven weeks.
04

05

06   *Fin.*

07

08

09

10

11

12

13

14

15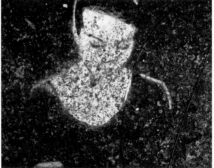

16

17

18

12 Friday Vendredi   *Week 6*

01 Valentine's Day is this weekend. You would think there would be
more Valentine hoopla. In the United States, you can't walk into
02 the pharmacy without getting accosted by bright pink Valentine
paraphernalia. You would think Valentine's Day would be some grand
03 thing here in the City of Amour. Aside from a few chocolate shops
with heart-shaped sweets, and flowers shops bulking up on inventory,
04 there was little fanfare. I expected parades, balloons, and dare I say
it, valentines. But as I walked hand in hand with Christophe along
05 the Seine today, I noticed the boardwalk was filled with couples
also walking hand in hand, lingering under bridges, kissing against
06 walls. There may have been a parade of sorts after all, one that
happens all year long in Paris.

07

08

09

10

11

12

13

14

15

16

17

18

15 Monday Lundi   *Week 7*

01 Nothing quite stirs up emotion, nostalgia, and romance like a
    walk along one of the many bridges of Paris. All are unique. All
02 have their own story. Napoléon built a few. The stones of the
    destroyed Bastille were used to build another. There is also a
03 bridge for making wishes and another for lovers to add locks and
04 toss the keys into the water as a symbol of commitment or to
    make a memory or something. Christophe and I haven't bothered,
05 preferring instead to partake in another tradition of sharing
    a bottle of wine at a riverside bench and watching the boats
06 putter along. The symbol of Paris is a boat. You'll see it on the
07 coat of arms, government buildings, schools, and stamps. The
                            symbol comes with the motto
                        fluctuate nec mergitur, translated:
               "Tossed by the waves but refuses to sink."

08

10

11

12

13

14

15

16

17

18

ST. JULIENNE DAY

16 Tuesday Mardi

01

02

03

"Along each side where earlier bridges had
houses, the New Bridge featured instead
spaces reserved for pedestrians; they
were raised in order to exclude vehicles
and horse traffic. We would call them
'sidewalks'; they were something that had
not been seen in the West since Roman
roads and something that had never been
seen in a Western city. Add this to the
fact that Pont Neuf was the first bridge
whose entire surface was paved, as all
the new streets of Paris soon would be,
and it's easy to see why pedestrians saw
themselves for the first time as kings of
the river."

—Joan DeJean, *How Paris Became Paris*

04

05

06

07

08

09

10

11

12

13

14

15

16

17

18

17 Wednesday Mercredi

01

The Zouave

02

A recent report revealed that the city isn't prepared for a major
03 flooding of the Seine. As the flood levels rose in 2016, the city
swallowed nervously. To add further angst, another bigger flood is
04 not a question of IF but WHEN. *Fantastique.* The Zouave statue
stands at the water's edge of the Pont de l'Alma. He is a soldier
05 of the North African infantry, one of France's most decorated
06 regiments. When the water level covers his feet, the river is
closed. At the *café,* I heard a man joke that the water might
07 soon reach his "cannon and balls." It reached his shoulders in 1910.

08

09

10

11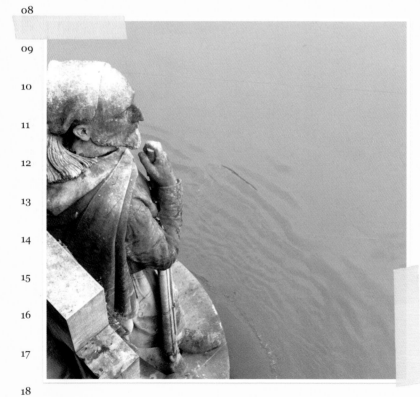

12

13

14

15

16

17

18

Pont de l'Alma, 75008

01

Nautical Hints around Town

02

03

04

05

06

07

08

09

10

11

12

13

14

15

16

17

18

19 Friday Vendredi   *Week 7*

01

02
"The time-worn stones were cold and the ever-flowing stream
beneath the bridges seemed to have carried away something of

03
their selves, the charm of awakening desire, the thrill of hope
and expectation. Now they were all in all to each other, they

04
had forgone the simple happiness of feeling the warm pressure of
their arms as they strolled quietly along, wrapped, as it were, in

05
the all-enveloping life of the great city."

06
—Émile Zola, L'Oeuvre

07

08

09

10

11

12

13

14

15

16

17

18

22 Monday Lundi   *Week 8*

01 # Anaïs Nin's Birthday

02 Yesterday was Anaïs Nin's birthday. She lived in Paris with her
husband Hugo in the 1920s. They rented an apartment where she
03 found a stash of erotic literature. As she began to read, she started
to yearn for something more than what Hugo could provide. In walks
04 Henry Miller. Their literary friendship bloomed into a love affair that
05 lasted years. When they weren't together, they wrote each other
passionate letters of desire, anger, betrayal, and love.

06

07

08

09

10

11

12

13

14

15

16

17

18

61, rue des
Archives,
75003

ST. LAZARE DAY

23 Tuesday Mardi   *Week 8*

01 As I look over the apartments of Paris, I wonder who is out
there now experimenting with a more modern love. What may be
02 tucked away behind the doors? An ornate staircase? A secret
03 garden? A secret love affair? A love child? Masterpiece in
progress?

04

05

06

07

08

09

10

11

12

13

14

15

16

17

18

24 Wednesday Mercredi

Week 8

01

02

03

04

05

06

07

08

09

10

11

12

13

14

15

16

17

18

"Was all this so wonderful because it was brief & stolen?"

—Henry Miller, in a letter to Anaïs Nin

ST. ROMÉO DAY

01

02

Renoir's Birthday

03

04 I first came upon Renoir in the mall when
I was a kid. His paintings were made into

05 prints and were for sale at one of those
makeshift stores in the middle aisle. Right

06 along side the discount books. I remember
thinking this was not the place for these

07 paintings. Then I arrived in Paris and saw the

08 original paintings at Musée d'Orsay. Ahh yes,
this revamped train station along the Seine,

09 glorifying the Impressionists . . . this is where
one needs to see a Renoir.

10

He began painting on porcelain, then fans,

11 and eventually canvas. Wouldn't it be lovely to
fan yourself with a Renoir?

12

"If you paint the leaf on a tree without

13 using a model, your imagination will only supply

14 you with a few leaves; but Nature offers
you millions, all on the same tree. No two

15 leaves are exactly the same. The artist who

paints only what is in his mind must very soon

16 repeat himself."

—Renoir

17

18

Musée d'Orsay, 1, rue de la Légion d'Honneur, 75007

01

Victor Hugo's Birthday

02

03 Victor Hugo's masterpiece, *Les Misérables*, has been on TV around the clock this week. They are celebrating Monsieur Hugo's

04 birthday as well as the debut of the latest film version starring Hugh Jackman. The story takes place during the June Rebellion

05 of 1832 even though many get confused and assume it's about the French Revolution, which happened thirty years earlier. In fact,

06 he was caught in some crossfire during the June Rebellion, which

07 inspired the story. Deciphering between the Revolution and the Rebellion can be as

08 confusing as deciphering between the Napoléons.

09 Yes, there are two. Strangely, the people

10 WON the French Revolution and LOST

11 the June Rebellion, but that still doesn't

12 clue in some fans once

13 the credits roll.

14   When Hugo published

15 the book, he sent a single-character

16 telegram to his publisher, asking "?" to which

17 the publisher replied with a single "!".

18

BOMBE D'AVION
30 JANVIER
1916

Air bombs: Also did not happen during the French Revolution.

29 Monday Lundi   *Week 9*

01
Napoléon B vs. Napoléon III

02
Everyone kind of knows and kind of doesn't know which Napoléon
03
did what in Paris. There were two and they are related. Even
locals skirt the issue. Who was the emperor and who was the
04
architectural mastermind? There are statues of one, or is it the
other? Who was in Waterloo? And when we see the "N" engraved
05
in bridges and on buildings, which Napoléon is it for?

06

07

08

09

10

11

12

13

14

15

16
42, rue Bonaparte, 75006

17

18

ST. AUBIN DAY

1 Tuesday Mardi   *Week 9*

01

Napoléon Bonaparte Cheat Sheet

02
* Emperor of France

03
* Tomb located in Musée de l'Armée, the national military museum

04
  of France at 129, rue de Grenelle, 75007

* The N on bridges and buildings is for this Napoléon

05
* Lost at Waterloo

06
* Posed with his hand in his waistcoat

* Did not have an itchy skin disease. His hand was in the shirt

07
  because it was the style

08
* Wore the funny hat (also the style)

* The statues you see around Europe

09
  are of this guy

10
* Chocked the Louvre full of

  art he picked up when his army

11
  swept across the Continent

12
* Lived in the Tuileries, just

  across the garden from

13
  the Louvre

14
* Considered bigger deal of the

  two Napoléons

15

16

17

18

2 Wednesday Mercredi

Week 9

Napoléon III Cheat Sheet

This was the Napoléon that lived at the Louvre. He was the nephew and godson of Napoléon Bonaparte, and was elected president of France. He is most known for his reconstruction of Paris. He had the vision to take the ramshackle medieval city and transform it into the grand dame it is today. Some people think he ruined it. But if you've ever lived in a city that grew without any big planning, you'll appreciate his vision. He was the muscle behind the cream and blue bourgeois apartments, the bridges, and grand boulevards. He hired Baron Haussmann to build it all. These streets "happened" to be wide enough for the government to flex its military muscle on the people. You can't erect ramparts across a big boulevard. You can, however get your front line down it in one dramatic march. The design made the city elegant and allowed the government greater control.

3 Thursday Jeudi

01

But the Best Part
About Napoléon III ...

02

03

04   He eliminated famine in France by modernizing agriculture and
making France a large export country. With the exports, France
flourished. Consider this the next time you open a bottle of
French wine.

05

06   Pas mal, as they say in France. Not bad.

07

08

09

10

11

12

13

14

15

16

17

18

ST.CASIMIR DAY

01

Paris in March is still naked.

02

    There is still no sign of the sprouting greenery or

03   blooming trees. The nude branches reveal what hides

behind them during more flamboyantly foliaged months.

04

    So far, it's 50 shades of neutral around here.

05

06

07

08

09

10

11

12

13

14

15

16

17

18

7   Monday Lundi   *Week 10*

01

     On the one hand, the gray skies are quite pretty—matching the

02   tightly regulated palette of the buildings' creams, whites, and shale.
But on the other hand, it makes one yearn for an early spring.

03

04

05

06

07

08

09

10

11

12

13

14

15   "And God knows, when spring comes to Paris the humblest
mortal alive must feel that he dwells in paradise."

16   —Henry Miller, *Tropic of Cancer*

17

18

8   Tuesday Mardi   *Week 10*

01   Of course, the French think of everything. So just while we are aching for spring to blossom, florists wheel out the hyacinth bulbs.

02   We buy them and force them to open early on our windowsills.

These are like alms, offered up to the Sun God to invoke warmer

03   days. And slowly, very slowly, the sun pokes through the clouds,

04   waking the trees from their winter slumber.

05   For a moment today, the sun burst through. People claimed the nearest seat, closed their eyes, aimed their faces toward the sun,

06   and grinned. It was a glorious moment. An hour later we were back to being shrouded in shade and life continued on at a glum pace.

07

14   "It's spring fever. That is what the name of it is. And when

15   you've got it, you want—oh, you don't quite know what it is you do want, but it just fairly makes your heart ache, you want it so!"

16   —Mark Twain, *Tom Sawyer, Detective*

17

18

9 Wednesday Mercredi

01

02

Paris Is Ours

03

The sun, like the students, must have zipped off to the Alps for March break. All that remain are locals quietly going about their lives in a Paris that is all their own. This week in March is quiet, calm, and ours.

04

05

06

07

08

09

10

11

12

13

14

15

16

17

18

10 Thursday Jeudi

01
Stamps & Covered Galleries

02 The covered galleries are a labyrinth of streets covered by glass
03 so you can shop and dine on even the coolest days. The stores are
a true treasure trove; full of antiques, books, artisanal bakeries
04 and hip restaurants. You'll also find a healthy handful of stores for
stamp collectors. I spent the rainy afternoon sifting through stamp
05 collections. I left with a big box of philatelic goodies.

06

55, Passage des Panoramas, 75002

11 Friday Vendredi

01   I had found an entire collection of First Day covers from the early 1970s.

02 These are envelopes that are released the first day of the stamp's release. It

03 shows the stamp, the official canceling

04 stamp, and a picture of the person, place, or event being remembered.

05   You can learn so much French history just by

06 investigating their stamps. For instance, the lady on the regular "Marianne" stamp was never a real person, but a

07 symbol of liberty in the French Revolution. She was named after the two most popular names of the day: Mary and Anne.

08

09

10

11

12

13

14

17

18

Having a woman to symbolize the liberty of France was also a way to visually break from the all-king oppressive monarchy. Each new president chooses a new design. The latest stamp is said to be modeled after a feminist. When she heard, she remarked that now the haters would have to lick her backside when they post letters.

    Charming lady.

14 Monday Lundi

01

02

03

04

05

06

07

08

09

10

11

12

13

14   * Passage des Panoramas: rue Saint-Marc, 75002

15   * Galerie Vivienne: 4, rue des Petits-Champs, 75002

16   * Passage Jouffroy: 9, rue de la Grange-Batelière, 75009

17   * Passage du Grand Cerf: 145, rue Saint-Denis, 75001

18

15 Tuesday Mardi   *Week 11*

01 The French love bits of paper. They adore saving postcards, collecting stamps, shuffling reports, and photocopying documents.

02 Many spend entire careers just moving papers around. Years later, these bits of paper end up in flea markets where they are sold to

03 other French people collecting more bits of paper. The home *décor* TV shows even feature big bookshelves of binders for people to

04 neatly collect their papers. It's either a collective love of paper or

05 a collective neurosis. I'm not sure which.

06
07
08
09

10
11
12
13
14
15
16
17
18

16 Wednesday Mercredi

Week 11

01

02

03

04

05

06

07

08

09

10

11

12

13

14

15

16

17

18

Le Parapluie

At this time of the year, you rethink your umbrella. Chances are, you've been wooed by a new spring coat on display at the grand department store Galeries Lafayette, and you realize your old umbrella just won't work with the new coat. Today, I zipped off to Parapluies Simon, which has been in the umbrella business since 1897. Inside were vases holding bouquets of pretty parasols, shelves stocked with folding *parapluies*, and ladies testing the release button on various umbrellas. In Paris, an umbrella is as important as your wallet, and you're willing to pay big bucks for an umbrella with a decent release, otherwise you'll find yourself battling to open said umbrella when the clouds roll in. And it rains so often that you'll curse the day you were too cheap to invest in the better brolly. You'll also want a high-tech spine that doesn't break with the first big gust of wind, lest your umbrella joins the army of broken and bent umbrellas that crawl along the quay like an army of spiders with broken legs.

Parapluies Simon, 56, boulevard Saint-Michel, 75006

17 Thursday Jeudi   *Week 11*

01

It's satisfying to note that St. Patrice Day in France is on the same
02 day as St. Patrick's Day in Ireland. This isn't always the case, which
confuses expats who pay close attention to name days.

03

The gray skies opened again today. In France, they don't have the
04 expression "April Showers." Instead the have, "*les giboulées de mars,*"
translated as The Downpours of March.

05

06

18

18 Friday Vendredi   *Week 11*

01
Macaron Day

02 Around the third week of March, France celebrates its prettiest
03 cookie. Participating macaron shops donate proceeds from that day to
charity. It's very easy to be in a very giving mood on Macaron Day.

04
05 "The macarons, though only a few grams, agitate our senses. The
eyes have already devoured them. Fingers skim their surface, the
06 flavors are gently smelled. When their fine crunchy shell is crushed,
the ears are excited by the sound. Then the mouth experiences a
07 delicate grace...."
—Pierre Hermé, famed pastry chef and founder of Macaron Day

08

0

1(

11

12

13

14

15

16

17

18

21 Monday Lundi

01

02

03

04

05

06

07

08

09

10

11

12

13

14

15

16

17

18

Le Macaron

The macaron consists of two cookies held together by a decadent filling. My first experience with this treat was at Ladurée. I walked in and saw a rainbow of macarons piled to perfection. Customers yelled out orders, "Vanille, chocolat, pistache!" and the staff neatly tucked each macaron into pretty pastel boxes. When it was my turn to order I panicked, pointed, and ordered what I could pronounce. "Café, vanille, citron…" Soon I was back on the street with my jewelry box of deliciousness. I meant to have only a bite of one or two. This was food to relish, not merely ingest, but soon I ingested the whole box. They are pricey so I researched how to make them. There is mixing and timing, and even weather conditions to consider. Humidity will crack the shell, which is unacceptable. Beauty is also a necessary ingredient. This dessert is half art, half food. Then there is the filling. The buttercream, ganache, or fruit filling must be stiff enough to keep the cookie together but soft enough to melt in the mouth. Oh bother! Realizing the mastery involved I decided to leave it to the professionals and only buy one at a time—or three.

22 Tuesday Mardi

01

02

03

04

05

06

07

08

09

10

11

12

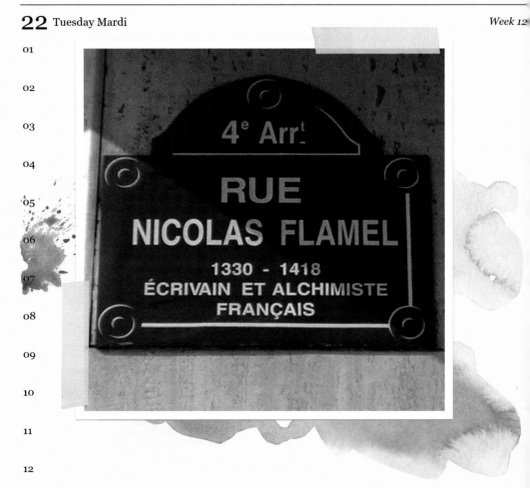

13 On this day in 1418 Nicolas Flamel died. He was a writer and an
14 alchemist who was believed to have discovered how to make gold.
Legend says he also discovered the Philosopher's Stone, which
15 made the holder of the stone immortal. Obviously this didn't work
out, as he proved on this day in 1418. He and his stone were
16 mentioned in the *Harry Potter* series by J. K. Rowling. He was
also cited as the Grand Master of the Priory of Sion in the book,
17 *The Da Vinci Code*, by Dan Brown.

18

23 Wednesday Mercredi   *Week 12*

01

02

03

04

05

06

07

08

09

10

11

12

13
14
Speaking of *The Da Vinci Code*, in the story, the Arago Rose
Line is said to lead to the relics of Mary Magdelene. The true
use of the Arago Rose Line is to mark the Paris meridian, which
15
was a long-standing rival to the Greenwich meridian as the prime
meridian of the world. You can find 135 of these medallions
16
between the northern and southern limits of Paris. I found this
one outside Saint-Sulpice church . . . the church that featured
17
prominently in *The Da Vinci Code*. Coincidence?

18

Inside Saint-Sulpice church you'll find a special line in the floor. This line was a big clue in *The Da Vinci Code* as to the whereabouts of the Holy Grail, but it's really just a fancy sundial, created to help the priests determine the exact equinoxes and hence Easter. At noon on certain days of the year, a ray of light shines through the window and lands on the brass line.

12

13   Contrary to what it says in *The Da Vinci Code*, the line does not mark the remains of a pagan temple. It was never called a "Rose Line," nor does it coincide with the meridian that runs through the
14 middle of Paris. See, people were getting this line mixed up with the
15 Arago disks. And getting a fictional caper mixed up with reality. There is also a P and S in opposite windows of the church. These refer to
16 Peter and Sulpice, not "Priory of Sion." The church was downright annoyed when throngs of moviegoers showed up.
17

    The whole thing reeks of intrigue.

18

Saint-Sulpice, 2, rue Palatine, 75006

ANNONCIATION

25 Friday Vendredi

01

All this talk of the Rose Line got me thinking of the
02 rose window at Notre Dame cathedral. Notre Dame
is named after Mary, the mother of Jesus, who, on
03 this day, got the shock of her life when the Angel
04 Gabriel came down to tell her she was pregnant with
the baby who was going to save the world and lead
05 us all to immortality. Not unlike Nicolas Flamel and his
immortal Philosopher's Stone, who, as we mentioned,
06 did not. Or Harry Potter, come to think of it, who
07 was also destined to save us all from evil.

08

09

10

11

12

13

14

15

16

17

18

28 Monday Lundi

01 Notre Dame is over 850 years old. A few years ago, she had a
power wash and centuries of black soot were removed. She now
02 glows as the reigning Gothic masterpiece of our age. Because
you're not worth a pilgrim's time if you don't house a relic of a
03 saint's finger or vial of blood, Notre Dame acquired the ultimate
relic: the crown of thorns. On Good Friday, during the service you
04 can put your head inside the crown. Sort of. It sits on a pillow and
you bow over it. Anyone can do it, and it's free. They also perform
05 this service other times of the year, but on Good Friday it feels
like it counts for more. Also on Good Friday, the bells of the
06 cathedral are silent. Legend says the bells grow wings
and fly to Rome for an Easter blessing by the pope.
07 On Easter Sunday, they return, dropping chocolates
all over France for the children.
08 *Bonne Pâques!*

09

10

11

12

13

14

15

16

17

18

01 When you climb the stairs of Notre Dame, it's easy to imagine centuries of monks climbing those same stairs to ring the bells. At
02 the top, you are rewarded with close-ups of the gargoyles. They sit, almost contemplative, watching the ruckus on the square below.
03 Up close, they seem like winged monkeys circa *The Wizard of Oz*.
04 Some believe their job is to ward off evil spirits and to protect those they guard. That may be partly true, but their real job is
05 to act as spouts so rainwater doesn't drip down the sides of the cathedral and erode the mortar.
06

07

08

09

10

11

12

13

14 Now I know these are mythical creatures. That there is no evidence that they ever roamed the earth, yet these creepy beasts
15 look so real and are seen on cathedrals at far reaches of the earth
16 that one can't help but wonder if they were once real. Perhaps they were pets of the Sasquatch, and their real job was to protect
17 the hairy big-footed man from being discovered.

18

ST. AMÉDÉE DAY

30 Wednesday Mercredi

Week 13

01 Even the graffiti on the roof of Notre Dame has an artistic flair.

02

03

04

05

06

07

08

09

10

11

12

13

14

15

16

17

18

01
02
03
04
05
06

07
08
09
10
11
12

13
14
15
16
17
18

Notre Dame Fast Facts:

* The bell named Emmanuel is the only original bell of Notre Dame. In Victor Hugo's famous book, the hunchback swings from this bell. The newer bells, which arrived for the church's 850th birthday, were tuned to Emmanuel.

* The city was going to tear down Notre Dame but Victor Hugo petitioned against it and he won.

* This cathedral is considered by many to be the best example of Gothic architecture.

* In front of Notre Dame is Point Zero of Paris. The city spreads out from this spot.

* The rose window motif is repeated all over Paris, including on the sewer grates.

ST. HUGUES DAY

1 Friday Vendredi   *Week 13*

01 While investigating rose windows and circles around town, three
round buttons popped off my coat. A trip to the haberdashery was
02 in order for new buttons. In French, a haberdashery is called a
mercerie and is one of the few words that sound better in English
03 than in French. It's a mouthful of glee.

04
     The best boutiques are around the corner from Moulin Rouge.
05 At the haberdashery, you'll find all the latches, buttons, ribbons, and
zippers you'll ever need to sew and mend clothing to invoke your
06 inner Coco Chanel.

07   You know a shop with the world's prettiest sewing kits is going
to distract you for much longer than it should. These, along with
08 boxes of buttons—silver, gold, ceramic, shell, and a rainbow of plastic
09 —are all available to solve any and all fashion emergencies.

10

11

12

13

14

15

16

17

18

4   Monday Lundi   *Week 14*

01   Coco Chanel once said "Dress shabbily and they remember the dress; dress impeccably and they remember the woman." A coat
02   missing three buttons doth a shabby dresser make.

03   I found gorgeous buttons that didn't go with my coat. In fact, I have NOTHING that would go with these buttons, but I considered
04   buying the buttons, then finding the coat. Or just buying the buttons
05   and framing them along with the original pretty packaging.

06   In the end, I found a set of eighteen vintage jewels to replace all the buttons on my coat, and I spent the evening sewing them on
07   with Cole Porter playing in the background. I felt like a glitterati of the fashion industry. I might have to re-button all my coats.
08

09

01
Coco Chanel

02

03 Often when I walk by Chanel on rue Cambon, I hear someone say, "I LOVE Chanel." I wonder how she would have felt having all

04 this admiration thrust upon her. She, of course, is worthy of such admiration, being the mastermind behind one of the world's most

05 recognized brands. She is said to have liberated women from the "corseted silhouette," for which I am thankful. If you've ever

06 squeezed yourself into a pair of Spanx, you know what I'm talking about. Shopkeepers at Chanel claim to have sensed her presence

07 in the store, usually during the quiet time after the store closes.

08 If I were Chanel, there is no place I'd rather haunt.

09   She also created Chanel No. 5, the most popular perfume in the world.

10 She says she came up with the name because it was the fifth scent she

11 tried and liked. Ever after, 5 became her lucky number. So it

12 should come as no surprise that when you walk into her flagship

13 shop on rue Cambon, you will see

14 a chandelier she had custom designed . . . made of iron

15 stamped into the iconic #5.

16

17

18

31, rue Cambon, 75001

ST. MARCELINE DAY

6 Wednesday Mercredi *Week 14*

01 But who cares about perfume when the trees are in bloom and their fragrance wafts by on the breeze.

02

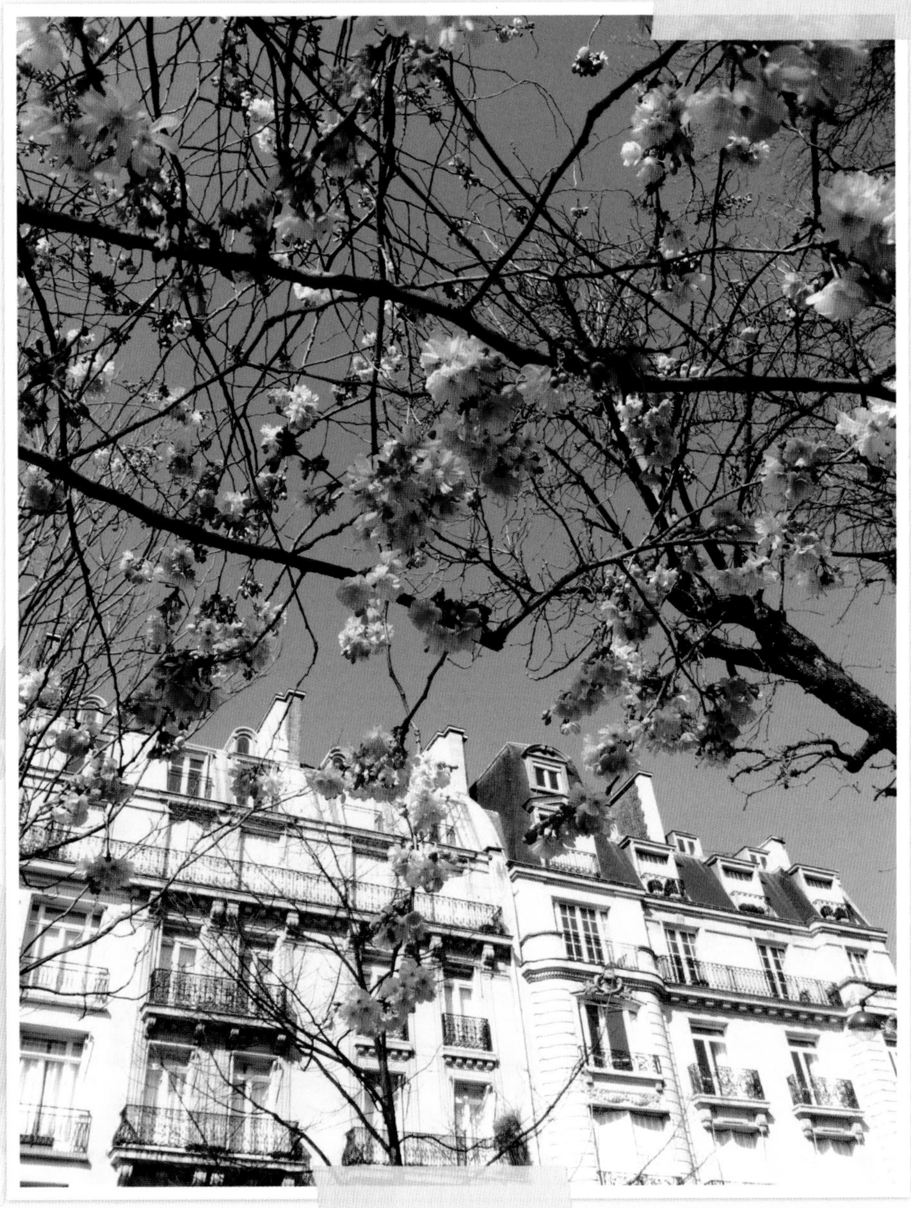

03

04

05

06

07

08

09

10

11

12

13

14

15

16

17

18

7 Thursday Jeudi

01 You truly notice the genius
02 of the arborists of Paris
once spring begins to bloom.
03 Boulevards burst with blooms
for miles, and monuments
04 seem framed by petals.

05 You also understand why
06 the gardeners post signs
in the parks, forbidding
07 stepping on the grass. They
know the daffodils and
08 tulips need time and space
to grow, and even the lawn
09 needs rest from time to
10 time.

11 "And so with the
sunshine and the great
12 bursts of leaves growing
on the trees, just as things
13 grow in fast movies, I had
14 that familiar conviction
that life was beginning
15 over again. . . ."
—F. S. Fitzgerald,
16 *The Great Gatsby*

17

18

8 Friday Vendredi   Week 14

01
Julia Child

02 The markets are just beginning to offer radishes, white asparagus, and strawberries. With the warm air, we tend to linger at the
03 markets in April. We no longer shiver through the stalls, choosing
04 just the essentials. We branch out, like those blooming trees, and try all manner of odd culinary curiosities.

05
06 Springtime at the market brings out your inner Julia Child. Today I bounded down my spiral staircase to walk in her footsteps along these ancient Paris streets. She started writing the
07 culinary go-to *Mastering the Art of French Cooking* here in
08 Paris in the 1950s. Many of those *boutiques* are still open and even run by the same families. That's how it is here. Family
09 businesses can last ages.

10

11

12

13

14

15

16

17

18

11 Monday Lundi

01 There are many Julia look-alikes in Paris.

02

03 After I bought her cookbook, I thought I could start whipping up amazing dishes for Christophe *tout suite*. Not so! I needed to read the book like a novel for a week, sending *mon amour* out to pick up Mexican food (I sheepishly admit) while I studied the merits of cast iron and copper.

04

05

06

07

08

09 Then I needed supplies. Not surprising, her preferred kitchen supply store, E. Dehillerin, is still open. When I went, I stood at the wall of spatulas and wondered what on earth to do with them all. I suspect Julia felt the same. So many kitchen tools. All keys to unlocking the mysteries of French cuisine.

10

11

12

13

14

15 She was a honeymooner at the time, just a few years into her marriage with Paul, who would wait patiently for her meals.

16

17

18

E. Dehillerin, 18, rue Coquillière, 75001

12 Tuesday Mardi

01   As I worked my way through her recipes, Christophe realized he would have to wait a long time before he had the pleasure of my
02 (Julia's) *boeuf bourguignon* and *suprêmes de volaille aux champignons* (chicken breasts with mushroom sauce). While I would read, stir,
03 and simmer, he would play love songs on the guitar. Paul sat in the
04 kitchen, too, writing letters. Julia and Paul lived into their nineties, which is considerable considering all that cream and butter. I hope to
05 do the same with Christophe . . . one scrumptious meal at a time.

06   It really is the butter that seems to elevate the dish. The butter in France is seasoned with the salt from the coast. Sauniers,
07 the salt harvesters, carefully rake up every crystal. Each morning,
08 they harvest the gray salt (*gros sel marin gris*). Gray from the nutrients embedded in the clay. By afternoon, evaporation on the salt
09 ponds causes the tiny salt particles to rise and float on the water. By evening they form a thin lacy crust. This is *fleur de sel*. It's
10 delicately harvested with special rakes, packaged, and sold off to
11 the nearest shop, chef, or butter maker.

13 Wednesday Mercredi

01

Typique Market Day

02

There is the gathering, gossiping, taste testing, deliberating,

03

deciding, carrying, unloading, displaying, chopping, mixing, simmering,

and finally, after all this, eating.

04

05

06

07

08

09

10

11

12

13

14

15

16

17

18

14 Thursday Jeudi

01

Non-typique Market Day

02 Generally, there are four types of markets:

03 *The usual grocery store: good for mustard, rice and such.

04 *Street markets: permanent outdoor markets that open Tuesday
05 to Saturday like rue Mouffetard, rue Montorgueil, and rue Cler.

06 *Open-air markets: These are like farmer's markets. Most
vendors aren't farmers but they know their stuff and are very
07 good at what they do.

08 *Artisanal markets: These pop up here and there around Paris.
Here you're buying directly from *les producteurs*. And this is
09 where I met the loveliest cheesemonger. He swelled with pride
when I asked to take photos of his cheese.

10
11
12
13
14
15
16
17
18

15 Friday Vendredi

01

This guy was a true artist. Some cheese looked wrinkled, some looked like dough, and it all looked good. I ended up buying almost one of each, more cheese than I could ever eat. One type was still "very alive" and he insisted I keep it in the cupboard and not in the fridge to let it soften. I was skeptical but a few days later, the cheese had turned into ooey-gooey goodness.

02

03

04

05

06

07

08

09

10

11

12

13

14

15

16

17

18

18 Monday Lundi　　　　　　　　　　　　*Week 16*

01 # Market Shtick

02 Routine is a valued trait on market day. Keeping to the script
03 allows us to revel in the changes in season. Same people, different
produce. Christophe and I have the same market shtick. He leaves
04 me cash for flowers before he heads off to the *boucherie* to roast
chickens. I stop by the shop on the way home from the flower
05 market and thank him loudly, *"Merci pour les fleurs mon amour."*

06

07　　The older
ladies in line sigh
08 and smile. Their
Christophe has love
09 in his life. This is
10 all they want. They
are like benevolent
11 parents, wishing for
the great happiness
12 of their children.
13 One lady admitted
that he is much
14 BETTER than her
ingrate children.
15 Each week the
16 same. Different
older ladies. Same
17 sighs and smiles.

18

119, rue Mouffetard, 75005

19 Tuesday Mardi   *Week 16*

01   Market day doesn't always go so smoothly.

02   There are long lines, petitioners shoving flyers in your face, and
the added pressure of speaking clearly in French when it's your
03 turn to order, unless you want the lesser vegetables, which you
will get by not speaking French. Will they understand me? Will I
04 understand them? Will I have wilted greens all week?

05   My friend Elsa stopped by her beloved flower market for her
weekly bunch of blooms. Elsa holds her extra weight on her belly
06 and admits to looking four months' pregnant, which she says is an
advantage on the Métro when a stranger offers her a seat. She
07   takes the seat and rubs
                                          her belly with affection.

ST. ODETTE DAY

01   Usually when you order something in French, the shopkeepers, sensing your accent, keep close to the script. It's cordial, efficient,

02   and friendly, as long as you start every conversation with a smile and a bellowing "Bonjour Monsieur" or "Bonjour Madame."

03

    Over time and with repeat visits, the shopkeeper might want

04   to advance the relationship and veer from the script. And this is

05   what happened on this particular day with Elsa. She had no idea what the shopkeeper was saying, but nodded politely, received an

06   enthusiastic response AND free flowers.

07   Confused, Elsa replayed the scene on

08   the walk home and realized her flower lady

09   thought she was having a

10   baby. And Elsa nodded in agreement. Embarrassed,

11   she now must either find a new flower vendor . . .

12   or a new baby.

13   Comedy gold.

14

15

16

17

18

ST. ANSELME DAY

21 Thursday Jeudi

01

One tree at a time begins to roll out the pink carpet for summer's arrival. C'est belle. C'est parfait.

02

03

04

05

06

07

08

09

10

11

12

13

14

15

16

17

18

ST. ALEXANDRE DAY

01   People are in the parks again. Pockets of color fill the city.
When one fades, another blooms. Makes you want to paint like
02   François Boucher. He was known for painting voluptuous ladies in
03   idyllic scenes.

04

05

06

07

08

09

10

11

12

13

14

15

16

17

18

REPUBLIQUE FRANCAISE   1,00 POSTES

F. BOUCHER

F. BOUCHER
18 OCTOBRE 1970
PREMIER JOUR
PARIS

25 Monday Lundi

01   Another artist who painted ladies in idyllic scenes was Monet. When he wasn't painting water lilies in his garden in Giverney,
02   which is just a short train ride from Paris, he was painting ladies
03   in pretty dresses. He claims he was influenced by the paintings of Eugène Delacroix. He also admits to often peering into the window
04   of Delacroix's studio to try to make out his shadow as he painted.

05

06

07

08

09

10

11

12

13

14

15

16

17

18

26 Tuesday Mardi   *Week 17*

01

Eugène Delacroix's Birthday

02

03 Eugène Delacroix painted, quite possibly,

04 the most famous French lady in an idyllic
scene when he painted *Liberty Leading*

05 *the People*. It's in the Louvre, where
artists like me can sketch art by artists

06 like Delacroix. The painting commemorates

the July Revolution of 1830, which

07 toppled King Charles X of France. It

08 features our leading lady, Marianne,
who figures prominently on the

09 French postage stamp.

10

11

12

13

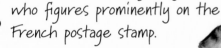

14 The boy holding two
pistols is thought to have

15 inspired the creation of
the character Gavroche

16 in Victor Hugo's

17 *Les Misérables*.

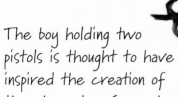

18

27 Wednesday Mercredi

01

Although the French government bought Delacroix's *Liberty Leading the People*, officials

02

deemed its glorification of liberty too radical so

03

they stored it away from view.

04

When President Napoléon III was elected, he had it put back on display at the Louvre for

05

sketchers like me to admire.

06

Decroix's painting must have influenced a few French stamp designers as well.

07

08

09

10

11

Degas was a fan, too.

12

He collected almost 250 of Delacroix's paintings

13

and drawings.

14

15

16

17

18

ST. VALÉRIE DAY

28 Thursday Jeudi   *Week 17*

01 April is National Card and Letter Writing Month
    in the United States, created to promote the
02 practice of letter writing. The French don't even
    need one of these commemorative situations. They
03 LOVE the mail. They love stationery. They love
    envelopes. They love stamps. In fact, they have a
04 special day devoted to the humble postage stamp.

05

07

08

09

10

11

12

13

14

15

16

17

18

29 Friday Vendredi   *Week 17*

01
Stamp Day

02 The postage stamp. The smallest,
most common piece of art. Framed
03 and promising.

04

    Traditionally on Stamp Day, a
05 special stamp about postal history
is issued. It's a celebration of the
06 philatelic arts.

07   Each year the post office also
creates a stamp for the Red
08 Cross (La Croix Rouge). Proceeds
go to the charity to help with
09 humanitarian aid.

10

11

12

13

14

15

16

17

18

2 Monday Lundi

01
May Day: La Fête du Travail

02 May Day is Labor Day in France, so everyone celebrates
03 the rights of workers, and oddly, they gripe about work in
demonstrations and strikes. Just as well it's a holiday as it's
04 impossible to get to work with all the demonstrations and strikes.

05　　　Everyone . . . and I mean everyone . . . who is looking to make a
few bucks, is out selling bunches of lily of the valley. Walking out
06 my door, I saw them all lined up. Every ten feet you could hear
them calling for you to buy their bouquets and no one else's.

07

08

09

10

11

12

13

14

15

16

17

18

ST. JACQUES DAY

3 Tuesday Mardi *Week 18*

On May Day you can sell without a permit. Many people become vendors on just this one day of the year.

01
02
03
04
05
06
07
08
09
10
11
12
13
14
15
16
17
18

4 Wednesday Mercredi   *Week 18*

01 I always buy my May Day flowers from the same Romani girl.
02 She always asks if I'm going to have children. She already had all of hers. She looks about seventeen. I don't ask. I just hand over
03 my coins and practice acceptance of other cultures.

04 My Paris is very different from hers. I go into shops, taste cheeses, and drink wine at the *cafés*. She would never sit at the
05 *cafés*. She would always stand just outside the world of those living in Paris.

06 After a time, the shanty village where she lives will be cleared.
07 That will be the end of my flower girl. In Paris, there are many fleeting relationships. Here one day, gone the next.

5   Thursday Jeudi   *Week 18*

01
Faire le Pont

02 Labor Day also, ironically, means now is the time to take vacation. You'll hear about *"faire le pont"* around this time of the year. This
03 literally translates to "make the bridge" and it means to bridge holidays. Since there are four national holidays in France during
04 May, and there is no school on Wednesdays, you can do some fancy
05 footwork accounting and end up with some very long weekends.

06   For example, if a holiday falls on a Friday, you can take a vacation day on a Thursday so you and the kids can skip town
07 from Wednesday to Sunday. Or tack on another couple vacation days on Monday and Tuesday, and you get eight days off for the
08 price of three vacation days. *Voilà!*

09

10

11

12

13

14

15

16

17

18

6 Friday Vendredi   *Week 18*

Robespierre's Birthday

It's also St. Prudence Day. If he had practiced more prudence and not cut off so many heads, perhaps he might have saved his own. He was the brainchild behind the Reign of Terror, a period of time after the French Revolution when nearly forty thousand people were accused of being "enemies of the revolution" and were executed by guillotine.

One of the last groups executed was a group of nuns who refused to give up their monastic vows. I'm not sure what this has to do with being enemies of the revolution, but it must have made sense at the time. They sang hymns as they walked up the scaffolding to their death. This had a great impact on the public mood and helped end the Reign of Terror.

My hairdresser Sylvie cut hair for years in the bedroom of what was once Robespierre's apartment at 400, rue Saint-Honoré. This fact astounds me, but she shrugs and states that Parisians are used to living with ghosts.

93

9 Monday Lundi

01

02

03

04

05

06

07

08

09

10

11

12

13

14

15

16

17 Sylvie has since moved her atelier to another address where no known mass murderers are said to have lived.

18

Sylvie Coudray Atelier, 6, rue d'Antin 75002

10 Tuesday Mardi

01

Le Foulard

02

With the first sunny day, we exchange our warm scarves for the

03

thinner "foulard" scarf. We pack away our boots and dust off our ballerina flats. And best of all, the cafés retract their walls to

04

let in the sunshine and warm breeze.

05

The French are experts at folding their glass-paneled

06

walls back. When they finally do, you know

07

spring has finally arrived to stay.

08

09

10

11

12

13

14

15

16

17

18

ST. ESTELLE DAY

11 Wednesday Mercredi   *Week 19*

01 If April's hue is pink then May's color is definitely bright green.
02 Some provided by nature . . . and some not.

03
04
05

06
07
08
09
10
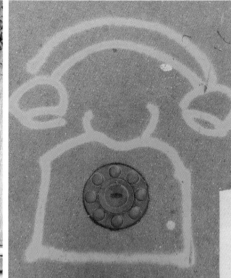
11
12

13
14
15

16
17
18

12 Thursday Jeudi

01   I'm not the only one celebrating the bright greens of May.

02

03

04

05

06

07

08

09

10

11

12

13

14

15

16

17

18

13 Friday Vendredi

01
Space Invader

02 Paris street artists are clever. The anonymous artist called Space
Invader makes little space invaders out of tiles and glues them all
03 over town. Finding one of these mosaics is like finding a hidden
treasure. I wondered how he did it until I was out walking early
04 one morning and saw a man fly by on his motorcycle with a ladder
05 strapped on the back. Could it be?

16 Monday Lundi

01

02 When you think about the concept behind
Space Invader's art, you see the brilliance.

03

A good story invites the audience to play along. Space Invader
04 and his cleverly hidden space invaders invite us to play his little
game. He also considers the placement of his little alien men. For
05 instance, Pigalle is the music district of Paris.

06

07

08

09

10

11

12

13

14

15

16

17

18

ST. PASCAL DAY

17 Tuesday Mardi   *Week 20*

01   A friend of mine came to town and thought the space invaders
were nothing more than junky graffiti created by a kid who likely
02   had a rough childhood. I don't see it like this at all. To me, he has
created art and used the whole of Paris as his canvas.
03

04   After a kitchen renovation, I had a pile of extra tiles. I often
looked at these square gems and wondered what art I could make
with them. Years later I see someone has solved this problem . . . and
05   I'm grateful it wasn't me. I wouldn't want to sneak around Paris at
06   night with a ladder strapped to my motorcycle.

07   Now you can find space invaders in cities around the world.
This one is outside Musée d'Orsay.

08

09

10

11

12

13

14

15

16

17

18

Musée d'Orsay, 1, rue de la Légion d'Honneur, 75007

18 Wednesday Mercredi

01

02

Jef Aerosol

03

Space Invader isn't the only graffiti show in town. Jef Aerosol is known for his black and white stencils, and his fun red arrows.

04

05

06

07

17

18

19 Thursday Jeudi   *Week 20*

01

Nemo

02

Nemo adds whimsy to many bland walls
with his cheerful balloons, umbrellas,
and man in red socks.

03

04

05

06

07

08

09

10

11

12

13

14

15

16

17

18

01

02 It's easy to see where the stencil graffiti artists get their
inspiration. The waiters show up in their black and whites each
03 day to serve up the hungry and thirsty. Around this time of year
04 I abandon my preferred *cafés* for those that are angled toward
the noonday sun. I hang my coat over the back of my chair, wedge
05 in at a small round table, and settle in for the main event—the
06 waiter.

Watching one waiter bust his
07 particular move is like watching a
ballerina. He swoops down to wipe a
08 table, swings around with a tray of
drinks, gracefully uncorks bottles,
09 explains the specials, gives expert
sommelier advice, and still manages
10 to sneak off for his break to lean
against a nearby wall to soak up his
11 own few rays of sunshine.
He is a true artist in motion.
12

13

14

15

16

17

18

23 Monday Lundi

01

TournBride

The best waiter in Paris is Didier at TournBride. He's kind, funny, and efficient. Plus, he just looks like that French waiter you believe in, minus the attitude. Being a waiter in Paris is a true profession. They go to school, are paid a good wage, and are a valued professional in the community. But all I care about is getting a few giggles in with Didier when I sit down to lunch. My friend Melanie once asked, "Do you want to hike across town, pay too much for substandard food, or do you want to avoid all that and go to TournBride. Didier is working tonight." TournBride every time, merci.

02
03
04
05
06
07
08
09
10
11
12
13
14
15
16
17
18

104, rue Mouffetard, 75005

24 Tuesday Mardi

01

02

03 Paris is an overcast town. So when the sun shines, we flock to
les terrasses and linger. Parisians are experts at lingering. They
04 don't order a coffee to go. They sit, sip, and stare off to the
street, scanning for familiar faces. The street is a catwalk and
05 it's nice to sit back and watch the show.

06

07

08

09

10

11

12

13

14

15

16

17

18

25 Wednesday Mercredi   *Week 21*

01 *Le Bistro Chair*

02 When you spend as much time in *cafés* as I do, you begin to notice that the *typique bistro* chair is like a snowflake. They are alike, yet
03 no two are the same. Surprisingly, one chair costs on average $500.

04

01
02
03
04
05
06
07
08
09
10
11
12
13
14
15
16
17
18

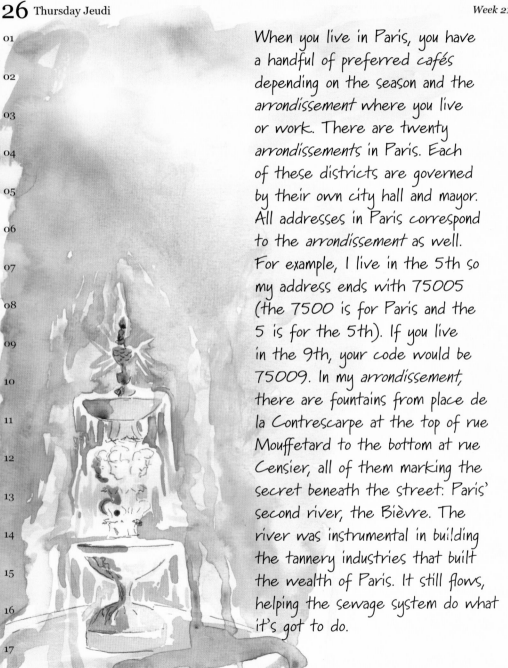

When you live in Paris, you have a handful of preferred cafés depending on the season and the arrondissement where you live or work. There are twenty arrondissements in Paris. Each of these districts are governed by their own city hall and mayor. All addresses in Paris correspond to the arrondissement as well. For example, I live in the 5th so my address ends with 75005 (the 7500 is for Paris and the 5 is for the 5th). If you live in the 9th, your code would be 75009. In my arrondissement, there are fountains from place de la Contrescarpe at the top of rue Mouffetard to the bottom at rue Censier, all of them marking the secret beneath the street: Paris' second river, the Bièvre. The river was instrumental in building the tannery industries that built the wealth of Paris. It still flows, helping the sewage system do what it's got to do.

ST. AUGUSTIN DAY

01

02 Outside the *boulangerie* at square Saint Médard, you'll find a
medallion on the ground, indicating that you're standing on the
03 ancient river. If you look up from that medallion, you'll find Café
Saint Médard, and this is the *café* where I work, wonder, and
04 watch the fountain gurgle.

05

06

07

08

09

10

11

12

13

14

15

16

17

18

30 Monday Lundi

01 # Café Saint Médard

02 People don't always take each other's phone numbers in Paris. They
03 just keep going to the same *café* at the same time as the same
people. Old-school style. They could have friendships that span years
04 without ever knowing each other's phone number or even last name.

05 As for me, I arrived very early to get in a good writing session.
My waiter hands me my *café crème* and we both get down to the
06 writing for the day.

07

18

53, rue Censier, 75005

31 Tuesday Mardi   *Week 22*

01

02

03   "A girl came in the café and sat by herself at a table near
       the window. She was very pretty with a face fresh as a
04   newly minted coin if they minted coins in smooth flesh with
       rain-freshened skin, and her hair black as a crow's wing and
05   cut sharply and diagonally across her cheek."
                                    —Hemingway, A Moveable Feast
06

07

09

10

11

12

13

14

15

16

17

18

1 Wednesday Mercredi

01

Le Rostand

02 But then there are times when you just happen to be across town
03 and need to eat. That's when I seek a writer's haunt. The city is
full of such magical places. I have a few for different purposes. I
04 have a *café* for my letter writing, a *café* for my journal writing,
a *café* for when I'm miserable and want to indulge in my morose
05 thoughts, and I have a *café* for book writing. (Sometimes those last
two *cafés* are the same depending on how the book writing is going.)
06 One such lovely writer's haunt is Le Rostand.

07

08

09

10

11

12

13

14

15

16

17

18

6, place Edmond Rostand, 75006

2 Thursday Jeudi

01

02 Le Rostand is a terribly well-behaved place mostly because
03 of people like me. Solo patrons looking for quiet in the midst of a
     midday hustle-bustle of clinking glasses and chatter of waiters.
04 The sea of patrons keep to themselves and sneak photos of each
     other. If we were to ever converse and share, we'd have an album
05 of lovely café shots of each other, but the first rule of Café Club
     is to never talk to each other.

06

07

08

09

10

11

12

13

14

15

16

17 A café is for "people who want to be alone
     but need company for it."
                    —Noel Riley Fitch, *Paris Café: The Select Crowd*
18

3   Friday Vendredi   *Week 22*

01 # Le Select

02 Hemingway made a habit of making certain cafés famous. He either went there to write or he wrote about them in his novels.

03 Le Select is visited by characters in *The Sun Also Rises*. They

04 hopscotched across boulevard du Montparnasse from Le Select to Le Dôme to La Coupole. One character describes Le Select as

05 "this new dive" because it was born with a bohemian grit.

06   Brown leather bench seats, dark

07 wood bar, grit and time have aged

08 this establishment

09 to a charming patina. While other

10 cafés in Paris do renovations to

11 appear authentically old, Le Select

12 stays true to its

13 roots. It's not changing a thing.

14

15

16

17

18

99, boulevard du Montparnasse, 75006

6 Monday Lundi

Week 23

Les Deux Magots

Another Hemingway hot spot was Les Deux Magots. He sipped legal addictive stimulants here along with intellectuals such as Simone de Beauvoir and Jean-Paul Sartre. Simone sat most mornings and wrote out her theories on existentialism and feminism. On occasion, Sartre would join her. They were scientists of the human experience and they used their relationship as a lifelong experiment. Early on, he asked her to marry him. She declined. They agreed to be committed to each other, in a way, by full disclosure about how they were feeling and with whom they were sleeping. They both had plenty of lovers, but Sartre once confessed, at times he couldn't leave the bed of his latest lover fast enough so he could meet Simone for coffee.

01
02
03
04
05
06
07
08
09
10
11
12
13
14
15
16
17
18

6, place Saint-Germain-des-Prés, 75006

7 Tuesday Mardi   *Week 23*

01   Their relationship experiment worked, it seems. They seemed happy and satisfied with their own definition of love for the rest
02 of their lives. Sartre died April 15, 1980, and Beauvoir died a few years later on April 14, 1986. They are buried together in
03 Montparnasse Cemetery in Paris.

04   Hemingway didn't have as much luck in love. He tried to adopt their open relationship ideals with his first wife Hadley and that
05 vixen Pauline. His desire for both the cake and icing resulted in
06 four broken marriages. Near the end, he admitted that the worst mistake of his life was ending his marriage with Hadley.

07

    Imagine, all these notions were infused with coffee from this one
08 café on boulevard Saint-Germain.

09   "When I saw my wife again standing by the tracks as the train came in by the piled logs at the station, I wished I had died before
10 I had ever loved anyone but her."
                                        —Hemingway, *A Moveable Feast*

11

12

13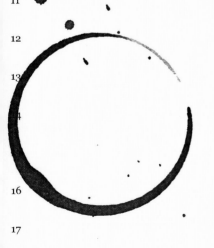

16

17

18

ST. MÉDARD DAY

01

02

03

04

05

06

07

08

09

Saint-Médard
Rue Mouffetard
Paris

10
Saint Médard

11 Saint Médard is the patron saint of weather. Legend says he gave
one of his finest horses to a peasant in need. Immediately afterward,
12 rain started to pour. An eagle spread its wings over the saint and he
13 remained dry while everyone else was drenched.

14 The French say, *"S'il pleut à la Saint Médard, Il pleut quarante
jours plus tard."* If it rains on June 8th, it will rain forty more days.

15

16 I live across from Saint Médard church so I hear the bells ring
all day long. I find it the the most pleasant way to predict, not the
weather, but the time.

17

18

9 Thursday Jeudi

01

Le Boucheron

02

03 There are certain friends you meet in certain cafés, based on their personalities, location, convenience, or just because they seem to match the café like people match their dogs. Le Boucheron

04 is where I meet the nomadic blogger. You'll come across a lot of bloggers in Paris. Usually expat wives who don't qualify to work

05 so they blog for something to do . . . and to subtly brag about their

06 expat lives . . . . But not my nomadic blogger. This guy was different.

07

08

09

10

11

12

13

14

15

16

17

18

14, rue de Rivoli, 75004

01 He zigzagged around Europe, blogging along the way, and
whenever he was in Paris, we went for coffee at this *café* in
02 the Marais, mid-morning, mid-week. Like me, he had quit his
corporate gig in the United States, and also like me, we were both
03 in Europe. Poor but happy. He survived on crackers, cheap wine, and
04 his wits.

05 We had met at Notre Dame. I was looking for the English
portion of the program. He was looking for a friend. He sat next to
06 me and flipped over the program to show me the English. Turns out
we both spoke the same language, which is all one really needs to
07 forge a friendship on the road. Afterward, we went for coffee.

08 He is a photographer, so we spent a lot of our time discussing
photography, developing, and cameras. It was he who pointed me in
09 the right direction when I was buying my new camera.

10

11 I always ordered my cream on the side when I was with him,
knowing he would drink whatever I didn't add to my coffee. He
was that poor. And he added a load of sugar before gulping it down.
12 Calories were counted as a survival tool.

13 Last I heard he was blogging outside a gas station
in Iceland, far away from that *café*,
14 hopefully getting by on more than
crackers, cheap wine,
15 and his wits.

16

17

18

13 Monday Lundi

Antoine the Poet

I am exasperated by my most recent quest to find Antoine the public poet. Antoine sits on rue Rambuteau in the middle of the crowds walking to the Métro. He waits for someone to whisper a word or theme in his ear and his fingers start plunking away on his old typewriter. I have made it my mission to whisper "Amour" in his ear so he could plunk out a love poem, but day after day, I've scoured the streets with no luck. I searched with such intensity that I was reminded of my own searches for love—the hot stress and the feeling of time being wasted, of feeling left empty-handed, of accepting that I might have to go without. As for Antoine, he's likely soaking up sunshine in Marseille, writing pithy love poems along the old port for tourists and fishermen. Perhaps one day he will return to conjure a poem for me.

14 Tuesday Mardi   *Week 24*

01

Le Flâneur

02
June marks the official season of the *flâneur*, the person who
03 leisurely strolls the streets. The *flâneur* was the first urban
explorer. He has all the time in the world to take in the ebb
04 and flow of the day. In New York, you'll be bulldozed over by a
pedestrian trying to get by you if you dare pause long enough to
05 admire the architecture. In Paris, you're slowed by pedestrians
06 in front of you. There will always be someone in front of you, so
you yourself slow down. And that's when you notice the latest
07 graffiti on a side street.

08

09

10

11

12

13

14

15

16

17

18

15 Wednesday Mercredi

01

02

03

04

05

06

07

08

09

10

11

12

13

14

15

16

17

18

On the first hot day, ladies pull out last year's frocks, wrinkled but comfortable and cool. Men tuck their jackets under their arms. And everyone opts to walk rather than take the sweltering Métro. Paris truly is a walker's paradise.

There are treats to be found on every cobbled street and every boulevard. Bridges beckon to be crossed, flower shops burst with blooms to behold, and bookstores lure you in with the summer's hottest titles.

Of course I can't read most of them. The French words behind the covers are much more advanced than I, but the French have style and it's enough to just admire the beautiful books.

16 Thursday Jeudi   *Week 24*

01

Café Saint-Régis

02   The Saint-Régis is located on Île Saint-Louis. Each morning, people

arrive with their notebooks and computers to get in a good work

03   session before the bustle begins. The place is full, yet eerily quiet.

04   Everyone keeps their own company.

06

07

08

09

10

11

12

13

14

15

16

17

18

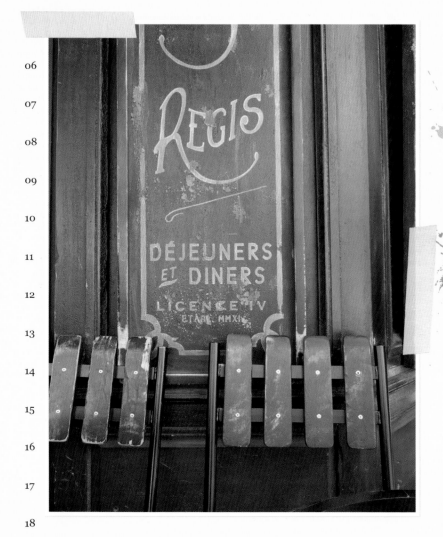

6, rue Jean du
Bellay, 75004

17 Friday Vendredi   *Week 24*

01
Le Petit Dejeuner

02 A sit-down *petit dejeuner* (breakfast) is rare in Paris. People eat
at home or stop by the *boulangerie* to grab something en route.

03

04

05

06

07

08

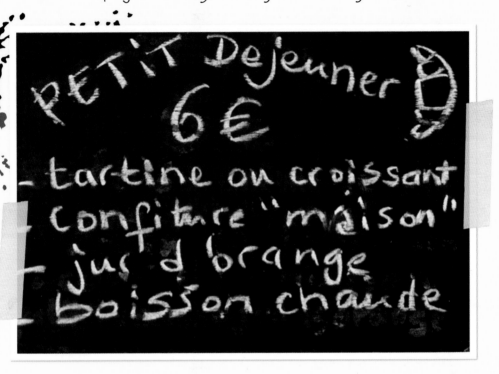

09

10

11

12

13   But the tourists in hotel rooms without kitchenettes need
14   to eat. They shouldn't expect a big egg breakfast. Eggs are
considered a lunch menu item, not a breakfast item. The French
15   breakfast is more continental: a bread, like toast or croissant, jam,
orange juice, and hot beverage are the basics.
16

17

18

01
02
03
04
05
06
07
08
09
10
11
12
13
14
15
16
17
18

The warm weather of June allows you to travel light, unencumbered by layers. Walks inevitably become longer. Today's walk took me to Musée d'Orsay to spend time in the Art Nouveau collection. Musée d'Orsay might be known for it's Impressionists, but they have an impressive collection of Art Nouveau as well. Art Nouveau was a design movement that took over the modern world around 1900. The style mimics nature. It incorporates the soft tendrils of vines and smooth curves of blooms into kitchen utensils, hair combs, advertisements, furniture, architecture, and fashion.

Across the river at the Petit Palais, you'll find an equally impressive collection of Art Nouveau. This movement had an innocence and gaiety about it, which was soon to be broken by the cost-effective straight lines of war. After I left the exhibit, I saw nature differently on my walk home. Instead of man-made items mimicking nature, I saw the opposite. Birds looked more like brooches. Flowers were more like hair combs. A climbing rose bush became an ornate iron balustrade. And vines that began to climb up the walls of my courtyard became the subject of today's journal entry.

21 Tuesday Mardi

01

Fête de la Musique

02 Summer in Paris is a carnival. The sidewalks sizzle, the cafés come

03 alive, and music plays all day long and into the night. Since this is high tourist season, many musicians are out busking for spare euros.

04 The one who catches my interest most is the accordion player who plays on rue des Gobelins. He has a sad pride about him—happy to be

05 playing but also tired. Though like any wind-up doll, he becomes more

06 animated when you plunk a coin in his cup. On the first evening of summer, Parisians celebrate *Fête de la Musique* when anyone with a musical instrument can play on the sidewalks of Paris without a permit and children are allowed to stay out late and run around like feral animals. They all drown out our accordion player and he fades into the background, but he waits it out and serenades the street alone later with a sad lullaby. He tells me has played since he was a kid. "It was my job. I had no choice."

07

08

09

10

11

12

13

14

15

16

17

18

125

ST. ALBAN DAY

22 Wednesday Mercredi

Week 25

01 
02
03
04
05
06
07
08
09
10
11
12
13
14
15
16
17
18

SACRÉ-COEUR FEAST DAY

23 Thursday Jeudi

01 Sacré-Coeur basilica sits atop the
02 district of Montmartre. This was
once outside of Paris and was home to
03 obscure artists like Picasso, Matisse,
and Van Gogh. They lived in this
04 bohemian fringe village not because of
the picturesque streets and stunning
05 views, but because it was outside of
06 Paris and therefore not subject to the
same tariffs.

07

08

09

10

11

12

13

14

15   Plus, the farther up the hill, the lower
16   the rent. A handful of nuns also made cheap wine here.
Cheap wine + cheap rent = artist haven. Artists still come here
17 and set up easels in the *café*-laden square *place du Tertre*. One
can buy a still-wet painting and wait for it to dry while indulging
18 in steak and fries at a nearby *bistro*.

24 Friday Vendredi

place du Tertre, 75018

01

02

03

04

05

06

07

08

09

10

11

12

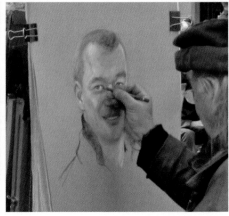

13

14

15

16

17

18

01

Sacré-Cœur basilica is constructed of travertine, stone high

02 in calcite, which acts like a bleach in damp weather giving the
monument its white appearance and making it look like a wedding

03 cake. It was built as a national penance for the defeat of France
in the 1871 Franco-Prussian War, and as a sort of punishment

04 for the Paris Commune. Somehow, slapping a giant church in the
middle of Paris' most rebellious district would bring order and fix

05 social and political issues. Kind of odd to wrap one's head around
that weird fact. It sits on the highest point of Paris, so even

06 though there are many steps up, and many pickpockets to

07 avoid, you can at least rest your weary legs in a pew.

08

09

10

11

12

13

14

15

16

17

18

28 Tuesday Mardi

01   But what I like most about Sacré-Cœur is standing in front
of it, turning around, and looking out over Paris. From here, the
02   city almost looks like a black-and-white photo. We can't see the
modern cars or mobile phone stores or burger joints. We only see
03   the Paris of a bygone age. The Paris we yearn for. And from this
view, we can pretend it still exists.
04

05

06

07

08

09

10

11

12

13

14   "Overall, I was happiest to be alone; for it was then I was
15   most aware of what I possessed. Free to look out over the
rooftops of the city. Happy to be alone in the company of friends,
16   the company of lovers and strangers."

17   —Roman Payne, *Rooftop Soliloquy*

18

June Juin

ST.PAUL DAY

29 Wednesday Mercredi

Week 26

01 Saint-Paul Métro is a popular place to meet up with friends as it's on the main drag of Line 1. I like meeting people here
02 because it's surrounded by cafés, which make for a pleasant perch to people-watch while reading texts from lagging friends.
03

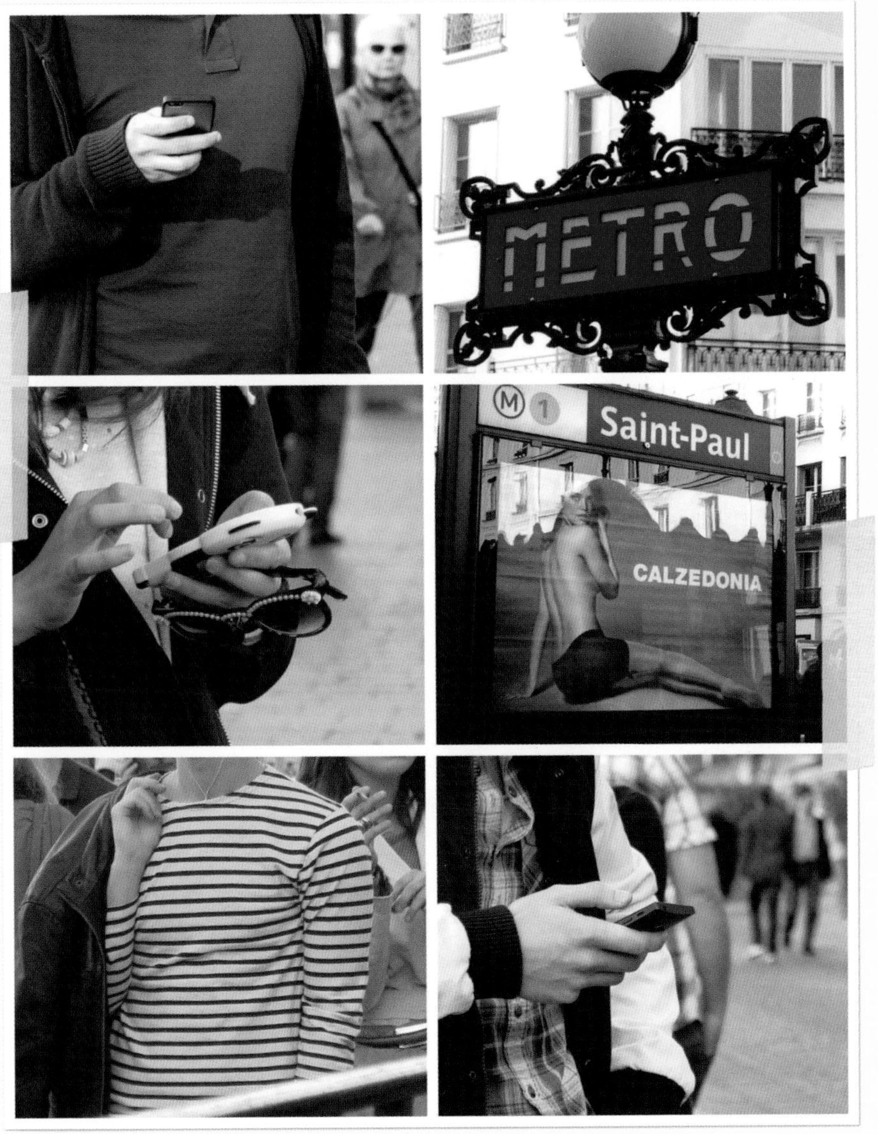

04
05
06
07
08
09
10
11
12
13
14
15
16
17
18

30 Thursday Jeudi   *Week 26*

01   Saint-Paul Métro is in the hip Marais area. Anyone who lives in the Marais assumes that if

02   you're not living in the Marais, you must be, in some sense, kidding.

03

04   It was here outside Saint-Paul Métro when I came upon Headless Pete and his hairy-armed

05   lady friend. Oh wait. Sometimes you have to look closer to see what's really there.

06

07

08

09

10

11

12

13

14

15

16

17

18

1 Friday Vendredi

01
Vélib'

02
Vélib' is a self-service bike system in Paris. You rent the bike

03
from one of the many stations, take your ride, then park the bike
at another station. The first thirty minutes are free, so the key is

04
to get where you need to go and park before you are charged.

05

06

07

08

09

10

11

12

13

14

15

16

17

18

4 Monday Lundi   *Week 27*

01   It's an odd feeling, to just leave a bike at a bike stand and
      never return for it. At first, you're not sure you're doing it right.
02   It goes against all your responsible bike-owner rules, yet once you
      get the hang of it, the feeling of leaving a bike and not having to
03   return for it truly feels liberating. The word Vélib' is a play on
04   bicycle (vélo) and freedom (liberté), and that's how it feels.

05

06

07

08

09

10

11

12

13

14

15

16

17   Sometimes the photography gods shine down upon you when you
      arrive for a bike and see that someone parked a perfect shade
      of car right next to the station.
18

5 Tuesday Mardi   *Week 27*

01 ## Versailles Schmersailles

02 If Marie-Antoinette were still alive, I suppose today would be her name day. People would wish her a happy name day all day long.
03 Most people don't know when you're birthday is, but they all know your name day. It's a wonderful way to feel special. To celebrate
04 her name day, I went to her small home in Versailles.

05   If she were alive today I imagined she'd be both chic and girly.

01 Everyone who has been to Paris tells you to go to Versailles.
They don't tell you why. "Just go," they say. So I went. And let me
02 tell you what they won't tell you: IT'S BIG AND KINDA BORING.

03 For a background, Versailles is where a bunch of the kings of
the Louis variety lived until *merde* hit the elaborately ornate fan
04 during the French Revolution. Now it's a tourist attraction. The
palace is ornate to the point of ridiculous. I mean, do you need a red
05 room, yellow room, blue room, green room, and teal room? Not to
mention a salon for the moon, Mars, the sun, Jupiter, and Saturn?
06 Non.
07

The place positively drips with chandeliers. But hey, when you're
08 a king and into being fancy, maybe this stuff is up your alley.

09

10

11

12

13

14

15

16

17

18

Palace of Versailles, place d'Armes, 78000 Versailles

7 Thursday Jeudi   *Week 27*

01 How to not lose your head in Versailles:

02 1. Comfortable shoes. It's big. Oh so big.

03 2. Take the tram to Marie-Antoinette's village out back where she would go to have that *faux* pleasant peasant experience.

04

05 3. Get tickets online beforehand. The lines are notoriously long and in full sun at Versailles, the home of the Sun King.

06
07
08
09
10
11
12
13
14
15
16
17
18

8 Friday Vendredi   *Week 27*

01   After a trip to Versailles you truly understand why the people
overthrew the monarchy. People were starving in Paris and Louis
02 was surrounded by gold in Versailles. The palace is actually outside
of Paris. You have to take the train. On the way home from
03 Versailles, we were stopped on the tracks for about an hour.
04 Who knows why. I was in the car with the African men who sell
trinkets to tourists. All day long they stand in front of Versailles,
05 rattle their rings strung with mini Eiffel Towers, and yell "One
euro!" Selling these without a permit is illegal, so they have
06 to outrun the police who come by every few hours. Then they
07 wander back when the coast is clear.

08   As we sat together in silence on the train, I heard quiet
sniffling across from me, then another sniffle a few seats over.
09 Many of these African men were crying. Big, strapping, handsome
men crying. I quietly chatted with one of them, the one who
10 offered me directions when I pulled out my map. He said they had
come so far, to this big Paris, to make money to send home to
11 their family. The idea is to arrive, make as much as they can, save
12 as much as they can by living in communal squalor for a few years,
then return home as the heroes of their families.
13

14 They must wonder at tourists
like me, frivolously complaining
about sore feet and long lines.
15 I'm no better than those royals
16 so long ago, ignoring the strife
all around me.

17

18

Au Petit Versailles, 1, rue Tiron, 75004

11 Monday Lundi   *Week 28*

Jardin des Plantes

This is how you stay cool on your run in Paris. Every morning, Jardin des Plantes opens its gates to early morning runners. There are two main shaded lanes. All of us run up one end of a tree-covered lane (top of the first), loop around at the end and head back down the other lane (bottom of the first), until our little baseball game is complete. There aren't many headphones with the early morning crowd. No sunglasses either. Just pure running, with all of us not looking at a clock or measuring progress. Just letting insights flow freely, solving problems and allowing inner calm to begin.

Jardin des Plantes is in the Latin Quarter, where many of the intellectuals in history lived. They say they lived here because the Sorbonne is here, but I wonder if all this running and walking is what really made the intellectuals intellectual. For me, I don't know how one could ever be a writer without also being a walker. Writing and walking are how a book gets done.

Jardin des Plantes, 57, rue Cuvier, 75005

12 Tuesday Mardi   *Week 28*

01

The Most Romantic Spot in Paris

02

03

04

05

06

After my run, I cool down in the rose garden just beside the lane where I run. It sits between the paleontology museum and the geology museum—roses tucked in between dinosaurs and diamonds. The bees are pleased to have the buffet of a million roses on which to feast. As you walk through the archways, you hear them buzz from above and you come out the other end knowing that whatever you brought with you to your run has been replaced by the delightful sound of drunk, happy bees.

09

10

11

12

13

14

15

16

17

18

13 Wednesday Mercredi

01

The Fireman's Ball

02 Part of my motivation for running in the park is to see the firemen.
Every morning, they run together in the park nearest their station.
03 They even have matching running gear. In France, being a fireman is
the ultimate profession, rating higher than even professional sports
04 players. Starting on the eve of Bastille Day, each fire station hosts
a Fireman's Ball. In the days leading up, they sell tickets around
05 town. I can't resist buying more tickets than I probably need.

06

07

08

09

10

11

12

13

14

15

16

17

18

ST. CAMILLE DAY

14 Thursday Jeudi   *Week 28*

01 ## Bastille Day

02 On this day in 1789, the resistance stormed the Bastille, which
symbolically marks the beginning of the end for the reigning
03 monarchy. Bastille Day started as a national holiday to celebrate the
French Revolution. These days it seems to be a day to celebrate
04 the military. The day starts with soldiers marching down the
Champs-Élysées with feathers in their caps—literally. The French
05 LOVE feathers. The pinnacle moment is when the Air Force flies
06 over, leaving a giant smoky French flag in its wake.

07

08

09

10

11

12

13

14

15

16

17

18

15 Friday Vendredi

01
02
After the parade, soldiers are "at ease" as they strut their stuff around Paris with medals dangling from their lapels. They often stop to pose for photos with children.

03

04

05

06

07

08

09

10

11

12

13

14

15

16

17
At the Bastille Métro station, the original fortress walls are marked on the platform on Line 5.

18

18 Monday Lundi

01

02

03

04

05

06

07

08

09

10

11

12

13

14

15

16

17

18

The *pièce de résistance* of Bastille Day was the fireworks show at the Eiffel Tower. This dazzling light show lasted nearly an hour. It was pyrotechnics of epic proportion. With some fancy light magic, they even made the Eiffel Tower sway, shimmy, and shake. It was marvelous. After the final firecracker cracked, I stood in silence with my friends, all of us hardly able to believe or discuss the wonder we had witnessed. Later that night, eyes closed in bed, sparks still danced behind my eyelids.

Bravo, Paris. Bravo.

19 Tuesday Mardi

01

Le Béret

02

All the military hats got me thinking about the *béret*. The *béret*

03
was originally worn by peasants, then clergy, then the military,
and eventually everyone. The traditional *béret* is a soft round cap

04
that is flat on top. The cap of the modern French man is a slight
evolution of the original round wool *béret*. Modern *bérets* are more

05
structured and less floppy. Personally, I like wearing a *béret* because

06
when it gets nippy you can cover your ears, then when it warms up
again, you pop the cap above your ears.

07

Instant air-conditioning.

08

09

10

11

12

13

14

15

16

17

18

20 Wednesday Mercredi

01   The *béret* has a timelessness about it. Layers upon ghostly layers pile up on the streets of Paris, stitched together with

02 time, history books, and the *béret* that makes an appearance in every century. And here we sit on the top, newer layer. But

03 really, it's not the top layer at all. Years from now another will walk on yet another layer, wonder back to these current days,

04 and marvel at what we don't yet know. And in that time, surely someone will be wearing a *béret*.

05

06

07

08

09

10

11

12

13

14

15

16

17

18

ST. VICTOR DAY

21 Thursday Jeudi

01
02 When you look at a creampuff from the Odette patisserie, you can't help but wonder if they've devoted themselves to creating the perfect béret in the form of a dessert.

ST.MARIE-MADELEINE DAY

22 Friday Vendredi   *Week 29*

01 Odette is one of the many mono-product shops in Paris that
devote themselves to perfecting one dessert. I don't know how
02 these places stay in business, but in Paris they seem to stick around.

03

04

05

06

07

08

09

10

11

12

13

14

15

16

17

18

77, rue Galande, 75005

25 Monday Lundi

01

02

03

04

05

06

07

08

09

10

11

12

13   There is this couple sitting at the café.
     He is holding her hand from across the table. She is sipping her drink and looking off in the distance. It's obvious she would rather be anywhere but here. And of course, her disinterest

14 makes him try harder, which makes her resist more. They are here on vacation together. The guidebook sits on the table next to

15 her phone. Is she waiting for a message from someone she'd rather be with in the City of Amour? Is she wondering about all the

16 decisions that brought her to this moment? Paris always seems like a good idea when tickets are booked, but unmet expectations of

17 the city or each other sometimes tag along for the ride.

18

26 Tuesday Mardi

01 *Cinq à Sept*

02 I see lovers quarrel all over Paris. It's a mix of jetlag, frustration
with the map, difficulty with the language, and fatigue by overplanning.
03 And that's just the tourists! The locals are mixed up in their own
quarrels, but those are usually based on affairs.
04

05 There is a dry cleaner in Paris called 5 à Sec, translated to "5
to dry." It's a play on the phrase *Cinq à sept*, or "5 to 7," which is
06 the affair you cultivate between leaving work at 5 and arriving home
at 7. These days, it's also used to describe a social gathering, or
07 what the English would call a "happy hour" or "wine and cheese."

08

JANICE MACLEOD

140 RUE MOUFFETARD

PARIS | FRANCE | 75005

RÉPUBLIQUE FRANÇAISE
1.00 POSTES

FRAGONARD

PARIS

PREMIER JOUR
22-1-72

"Never to go on trips with
anyone you do not love."

—Hemingway, *A Moveable Feast*

PAR AVION
VIA AIR MAIL

27 Wednesday Mercredi   *Week 30*

01
The Lost Generation

02 It was on this day when Gertrude Stein died in 1946. She was
an American author and art collector. She had the foresight to
03 buy paintings from the likes of Cézanne, Matisse, Picasso, Renoir,
04 and Toulouse-Lautrec before their art exploded in price. She
also often hosted the literary American elite at her apartment,
05 including Hemingway and Fitzgerald. I retraced Hemingway's steps
from his apartment on rue Cardinal Lemoine over to Stein's on rue
06 de Fleurus. A pleasant zigzag through quiet backstreets and Jardin
du Luxembourg, then onto her street where I spotted the usual
07 plaque that says someone important lived here. I can understand
08 why he liked the walk. It was just far enough to feel spent
and thirsty. This is what you do in Paris. You discover the Lost
09 Generation (coined by Miss Stein) and begin to study the authors.
They tended to use common themes in their writing, mainly their
10 experiences in World War I and the frivolous lives of the wealthy.

11 Then you read their memoirs
and retrace their steps until
12 you get the prize of arriving
at the beginning of it all: a
13 plaque on the building where
it happened. I don't know
14 why this is so satisfying
15 but it is.

16   "All of you young people
who served in the war.
17 You are a lost generation."
18   —Gertrude Stein

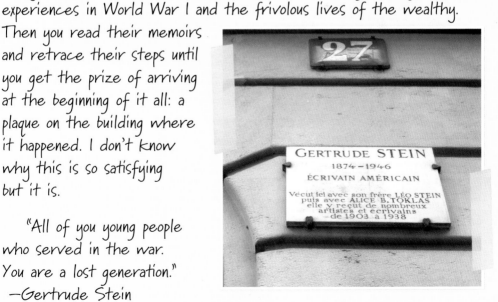

27, rue de Fleurus, 75006

28 Thursday Jeudi

01 *Bonnes Vacances*

02

03

04

05

06

07

08

09

10

11

12

13 I feel rather lost at this time of the year, as it's the beginning of
the big vacation. Most people leave Paris for four or five weeks,
14 starting at the end of July. There are so many businesses closed
for the month that it becomes difficult to find a decent baguette.
15 *Quel dommage.* Tourists that arrive in Paris at this time of the
year are missing the whole show. Doors are locked, shutters are
16 shut, and cute signs appear in windows explaining that if you came
looking for the Parisian experience, your best bet is to head to the
17 beaches in the south of France. Even the famous ice-cream shop
18 Berthillon closes for summer vacation.

29 Friday Vendredi   *Week 30*

01 The food markets are sparse and sad with most vendors not
bothering to sell in Paris when there is no one around to purchase
02 their food. It's at this time of the year when I sidle up to my
preferred cashier at the grocery store. Cashiers in Paris grocery
03 stores are, on the whole, grouchy. And that is truly putting it
04 mildly. If you don't give the exact change or hand over a fifty-
euro note doled out from the ATM, you will suffer their wrath.
05 It can take years to befriend a grocery store cashier. You have
to figure them out. Approach them like they are wild animals. I've
06 been working on befriending the cashier from Senegal. I think I've
07 figured her out. She is a wig wearer. When she's wearing her big
curly wig, you can approach with confidence. She's all smiles. When
08 she wears her serious office-lady bob, she's stern but fast. And
when she doesn't wear any wig at all, I just don't buy anything from
09 her that day. Her real hair is shorn like she did it herself in a gas
10 station bathroom. On one wig-less day, I saw two young American
girls attempt to buy something with a bankcard. Of course their
11 bankcard wouldn't work at the grocery store, but they didn't
know that. Once the card was rejected, she slammed her drawer,
12 grabbed the bag of groceries from the girl, then pointed at the
13 door with a loud *"Non!"* I turned on my heels and walked away.

14
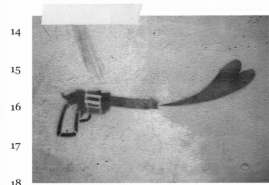
15
16
17

18

1 Monday Lundi

01
Waiting Game

02
A new person to Paris does a lot of waiting. First, there is waiting
03
in lines. After time, you learn to watch the locals. For instance,
before a service at Notre Dame, they open a separate line for
04
those attending the service. Hop in that line and you're in. Second,
you never, ever go to museums on the free day. Each big museum
05
has a day every month when admission is free. The lines go around
06
corners that continue to go around more corners. And once you're
at the front of that line, you realize you're about to enter a very
07
crowded museum where you will inevitably wait more to see what
you came to see. Just pony up and pay another day.
08

09

10

11

12

13

14

15

16

17

18

Tired of waiting at the Egyptian exhibit at the Louvre.

2 Tuesday Mardi   *Week 31*

01 # Waiting on a Woman

02 I befriended an American girl in Paris. Or perhaps she befriended
03 me. We were new in town and met at a Meetup group.

13 Meetup groups are popular in Paris and are usually well-attended.
14 You sign up online, then attend the event. Once you befriend, you
share information and meet later one-on-one. My American girl
15 would always meet me outside Chez Julien. Always twenty minutes
late, which is fine for the French, but it rubbed me the wrong way
16 coming from an American, who are usually punctual. When I decided
17 to bring my book along for the wait, she would be on time. I was
miffed again because I didn't get to read my book. It's challenging to
18 navigate between cultures.

3 Wednesday Mercredi

01

Colette

02 The famous French author Colette died on this day in 1954.

03 She wrote *Gigi*, the story of a girl being trained as a courtesan to become the mistress of a wealthy man, but she went off and

04 married him instead. The audacity! In 1951 Audrey Hepburn played Gigi on stage, chosen by Colette herself. Colette was equally known

05 as a cat lover. She famously started her working day by picking the fleas off her cat. Now, she lies in Père Lachaise Cemetery

06 in Paris, where feral cats likely meander around her grave.

07

08

09

10

11

12

13

14

15 "It's so curious: one can resist tears and 'behave' very well in

16 the hardest hours of grief. But then someone makes you a friendly sign behind a window, or one notices that a flower that was in

17 bud only yesterday has suddenly blossomed, or a letter slips from a drawer . . . and everything collapses." —Colette

18

4 Thursday Jeudi

01

02

03

04

05

06   Colette is a lucky lady. The cemeteries of Paris are full of cats. They all seem well fed. I'm not sure if that's because the cemetery caretakers also take care of the cats, or because Paris is chock full of mice and rats. I went looking for Colette, but all I found was a bunch of cats . . . and Édith Piaf.

07

08

09

10

11

12

13

14

15

16

17

18

5 Friday Vendredi   *Week 31*

01

Édith Piaf

02 Édith Piaf was a French cabaret singer. Her best known

03 international songs are "La Vie en rose, "Non, je ne regrette rien," and "La Foule." She is known to have sung on the streets

04 of Pigelle for pennies, and would go inside courtyards at night to belt out a tune or two. Residents of the apartments would

05 rain down coins to her. She was accused of murder, of being a traitor to France during the German occupation, and of sleeping

06 with a man so he would pay for her daughter's funeral. After a

07 serious car crash, she became addicted to morphine and alcohol. She died at forty-seven. The church didn't grant a funeral

08 Mass because of her racy lifestyle, but her funeral procession was attended by over 100,000 fans. Fifty years later, the

09 church changed their tune and gave her a memorial service.

10

11

12

13

14

15

16

17

18

Père Lachaise Cemetery, 16, rue du Repos, 75020

8 Monday Lundi   *Week 32*

01

02   The final words of Édith Piaf:

02

"Every damn fool thing you do in this life you pay for."

03

04

05

06

07

08

09

10

11

12

13

14

15

16

17

18

9 Tuesday Mardi   *Week 32*

01
Père Lachaise Cemetery
02
This, the largest in Paris, is home to a slew of celebrities. Two frequently visited graves are those of Jim Morrison and Oscar Wilde.

03

04

05

06

07

08

09

10

11

12

13

14

15

16

17

18

10 Wednesday Mercredi   *Week 32*

01 # Père Lachaise Insider Tip

02 The most ornate graves are on the main walkways, so if you feel
like you'll never see all the good stuff, stick to the main drag, and

03 you will have seen most of the good stuff. Don't forget to look
up. While you're off looking for Chopin and Proust, the staff are

04 actively cremating the newest members in the crematorium. Also,

05 because Père Lachaise is so old, the trees are huge, which means
the shade is plentiful. A smart choice for a summertime tourist.

06

07

08

09

10

11

12

13

14

15

16

17

18

11 Thursday Jeudi *Week 32*

01
Secret Sidewalk Artist

02 So I'm standing at the stoplight minding my own business when
I look down at the paint on the crosswalk and see someone
03 looking back at me. This street artist is brilliant, using the white
crosswalk strips as a canvas. Whenever I find one of these faces
04 I feel like I won a prize. This is a playful artist that rewards
05 those who pay attention.

06
07
08
09
10
11
12
13
14
15
16
17
18

12 Friday Vendredi

01   I don't know who this artist is but I know almost all of the
faces are found on the streets surrounding the Sorbonne. It's
02 likely the work of one of the art students. I've watched these
students sketch in parks and at *cafés* around Paris. Nothing
03 will make an artist feel inferior like watching a student at the
Sorbonne sketch something brilliant by the time their *café crème*
04 is down the hatch. I love pointing out the faces to out-of-town
guests. It's the ultimate surprise and delight.
05

06

07

08

09

10

11

12

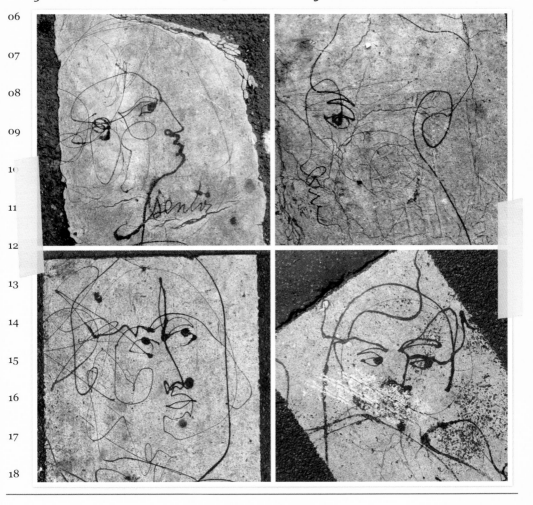

13

14

15

16

17

18

ST. MARIE DAY

01

Les Piscines

03 With the summer heat beating down, there is a renewed interest in the pools. Folks are eager to shed the *chèvre* and *brie* they
04 pack on the rest of the year. There are thirty-eight pools in Paris. Mine is "Piscine Pontoise Quartier Latin." It's an art deco
05 marvel with two mezzanine levels of private change rooms
06 overlooking the pool. The water is so warm I can't help but wonder if there is enough chlorine to kill off
07 bacteria. No one else seems to mind so I guess I won't either.
08

09

10

11 Everyone snaps on their swim caps
12 and quietly propels themselves back and
13 forth and back again. Speed doesn't seem to be part of the
14 value system of these swimmers.
15 Slow and steady are what these people believe in. I think this is what keeps them young. Paris is a mecca of older, healthy, mobile
16 people. Slow and steady seems to work, plus the emollients and creams they apply afterward in the shower. Goo galore slathered
17 on to keep everything in good working order for the long haul of
18 a life well lived.

Eiffel Tower

This is, for me, the best time to visit the Eiffel Tower. Unlike the *boutiques*, the big touristy spots stay open in August, but even they are subdued. The pickpockets, who usually swarm the tower, are on vacation, too . . . likely following the locals to holiday in Provence. Those who remain in the city have a respite from the "pushing through" required of Paris life during the rest of the year. In August, the lines are short and you always get a seat on the train. It's a time for long reflective strolls along the Seine, for lingering at *cafés* (again, you always get a good seat), and to revel in rare quiet moments in the cool shade of the Eiffel Tower.

17 Wednesday Mercredi   *Week 33*

01
Colin Was Cursed with Company

02 With my usual *café* buddies sunning themselves in San Tropez, I
03 sent a message to Colin for a sneaky midday beer. I knew he would
be in town. He never takes vacation in August. When everyone in
04 every office is calculating vacation days and scouring maps and train
schedules, Colin is sitting back and getting ready for a blissful month
05 of quiet. Colin is a confirmed introvert. A group of people is just a
bothersome brigade that makes him tired and spent. He is skittish
06 like a wild animal, but I have learned to approach him with caution.
07 He's not antisocial, but he prefers to visit with just one other
person, so on this particular day when everyone else was out of
08 town, we met at the back of a *tabac* shop called Les Facultés on
rue d'Assas because the name of the *rue* was too funny to not visit.
09 Over pints of beer, he told me how he came to live, and enjoy
10 living, in one of the most populated cities in the world.

11

12

13

14

15

16

17

18

01 Before Paris, Colin lived in London. He couldn't shake people from his daily life. He took great pleasure in solitary pursuits such
02 as reading, practicing guitar, and minding his own business. But this didn't stop interruptions. He worked in finance. Numbers. Not words.
03

04 Each evening he would stop for one solitary cocktail at the bar by his office. At first, a colleague joined him simply by following him
05 from the elevator. The next day, that same colleague met him at his desk and followed him down. Innocent enough. A rare coincidence.
06 Something Colin could manage on occasion. Word got out that there were drinks after work and soon five, then ten people arrived.
07

08 Colin could hardly confront the issue. He rates Not Being Rude high on his value list. He had no other choice but to transfer to
09 the Paris office where he hoped language would be an effective barrier. He found an apartment on rue des Bernardins. A quiet space
10 near Notre Dame and the river. And everyone in his building spoke French. Bliss.

11
12
13
14
15
16

17

18

ST. JEAN EUDES DAY

01   The problem with people continued on his first day of work. He woke alone. Dressed alone. Said good-bye to no one and was quite
02 pleased to do so. Or not do so in this case. He even managed to not run into anyone on his way down to the street.
03

    It started at Pont de l'Archevêché, the bridge littered with
04 locks behind Notre Dame. Tourists flocked here to "lock their
05 love" on this bridge behind Notre Dame. A local would never dare. It's simply not done. A couple who had just tossed the key into the
06 water stopped him and asked for a photo. He, not wanting to be rude, smiled a half smile, said *"Oui, bien sur,"* and complied. *"Merci!"*
07 they said as he continued on.

08   At Saint-Paul Métro, he gave his seat to an older woman
09 and she repaid him with conversation. He nodded politely but noncommittally. When he said, "Sorry, I don't speak French," she
10 continued in English.

11

12

13

14

15

16

17

18

22 Monday Lundi

01

02   He had to dodge crowds all the way to the office. People were everywhere. Even when they weren't.

03

04

05

06

07

08

09

10

11

12

13

14

15

16

17

18

23 Tuesday Mardi

01 Colin arrived in his new office not knowing anyone, and was
pleased with this fact, hoping he never would. Not so. The French,
02 it seemed, spent the first two hours of each workday leaning inside
the doorframes of offices making chitchat. What did they do last
03 weekend? What will they do next weekend? The gall of the
04 waitress downstairs who dared leave to give birth and leave them
with a substandard replacement.

05

These conversations would always, inevitably, disappointingly, lead
06 to lunch plans. Another two-hour affair of chitchat with colleagues.
He joined at first, realizing he was the shiny new bauble. He hoped
07 the shine would wear off and his lunch mates would regress to living
08 without his company and return to their established relationships.
Not so.

09

He could predict to the minute when one of his colleagues
10 would stop by, lean on his doorframe, inform him about lunch plans,
and ask if he would he like to join.

11

On occasion, he would
12 make the excuse that he
had prior engagements with
13 an out-of-town guest. Lies,
14 of course, but the result
was a blissful, quiet lunch
15 many, many blocks away.

16

17

18

01   Once he made the mistake
of telling someone he had a
02 medical appointment, but this
proved ineffective as the
03 French, it seemed, loved to
discuss medicine. A trip to the
04 doctor could entertain the
lunch crew for a week. And
05 eventually, the prior engagement
with an out-of-town guest
06 resulted in questions of who it
might be. Do tell. Is it with the
07 new girl in PR? *Elle est belle.*
08

09   And of course, the "too
much work to leave for lunch"
10 excuse he tried later was met
with disdain. The object of any
11 corporate employee in France
should never be to work harder.
12 "This isn't a sprint," one colleague
explained. "It's a marathon." So
13 the objective was to stay in a job
over the course of a lifetime,
14 which meant stretching the
work out as long as one could,
15 preferably interspersed with
long, lingering lunches marinated
16 in good French wine.
17

18

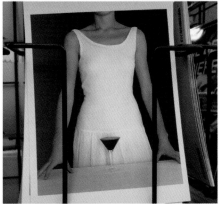

25 Thursday Jeudi

01   If he couldn't get peace at work, at least he had home. Until the day he missed a meeting and the condo board voted him

02 president. He accepted this position only because there was an unclaimed room beside the door of his condo, and he thought he

03 could more easily absorb the space into his own apartment if he was president. Less likelihood of questions. Wouldn't he as the president

04 be in charge of the questioning? No one even knew the room was

05 there. Who would even notice?

06   A little desk. A lamp. Books. Silence. No one else. Bliss.

07   While he worked away on carving the secret space next door into his home, he also carved away a secret space in his mind at

08 work. He fantasized for himself a sort of retirement job at the local bookshop. The antiquarian department. Rare books. Limited

09 editions. Forgotten tomes. That sort of thing. No one is interested

10 in such things anymore. It would be the one place he would be left alone. Genius!

11

12

13

14

15

16

17

26 Friday Vendredi

01   Not that he was qualified, of course, to deal in rare books.
Details. Ah, but he reasoned that his charming English accent
02   and his degree from Oxford would fool the French into thinking
he knew a thing or two about a rare book or two. He would
03
never admit his degree was actually in Finance and French. Once
04   comfortably hidden away behind his desk behind a lost art, he would
be free of the endless conversations. The constant droning of words
05   would cease. Words were like steps, each running into the next.
And he was burdened with the obligation to listen, to respond, to
06
stay present. But in his little nook in his little bookstore, he could
07   sit for days on end, entirely left to his own thoughts. Now that
would be bliss, he thought. That would be bliss indeed. And so he
08   continued with his marathon, group lunches, and Métro conversations.
As he stood nodding to the flapping lips, he dreamt of his silent
09
spaces, in the bookstore and in his secret room. Bliss. bliss indeed.

10

11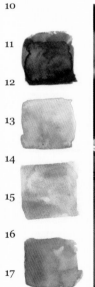

12

13

14

15

16

17

18

ST. SABINE DAY

29 Monday Lundi

01

"The only thing that could spoil a day was people and if you could keep from making engagements, each day had no limits."

02

—Hemingway, *A Moveable Feast*

03

04

05

06

07

08

09

10

11

12

13

14

15

16

17

18

17, rue de Beaujolais, 75001

01

02

03

04

05

06

07

08

09

10

11

12

13

14

15

16

17

18

Paris Keys

When the rental agent handed me an enormous brass key, it seemed like the kind of key that unlocks a treasure chest or a château. But no, she assured me. This was the key to my dinky little apartment. This giant antique couldn't possibly work anymore. Yet, the agent reminded me, "Old doors. Old keys," she said. "Don't lose it," she said, and pointed her finger at my nose. "Very expensive to replace." And off she went. The key did indeed work, and it got me thinking about how many keys are in Paris. Every door has a lock and each lock has a key. How many keys have been lost? How many are at the bottom of the Seine? How many people forget to leave their key, and fly back to their homeland with the key tucked in their pocket? And how many people have tucked the same key into their pocket to open the same doors for the last eighty years? It boggles the mind.

ST. ARISTIDE DAY

01 The key cutter on my street has been making keys in the same tiny shop off rue Mouffetard for the last fifty years. He,
02 himself, boasts that he has only used the one key to get into his shop. He also mends shoes, which is what brought me into his shop.
03 I showed him my key and asked him how old he thought it might
04 be. "That key? Not so old. Maybe sixty or seventy years."

05 The cheesemonger on rue Mouffetard is the official key keeper of the street. When someone leaves for a month-long
06 vacation, but will have work done on their apartment while they are away, they leave the key with the cheesemonger. I don't
07 know how he keeps the keys straight, but he manages. There
08 are no notes on the keys, no addresses, no names. He just seems to know.

09
Sure enough, when I returned from a trip, I strolled up to him
10 with my suitcase. He saw me coming and had my key waiting for me by the time I arrived. There is no payment for this service,
11 but I assure you, I bought cheese that day.

12
13
14
15
16
17
18

1 Thursday Jeudi

Week 35

01 ## La Rentrée

02

03

04

05

06

07

08

09

10

11

12 By now, most everyone has returned from their month-long
vacation in August. They call it *rentrée*. It's similar to "back-to-
13 school" but more pleasant somehow. During *rentrée*, shopkeepers
dust off the cobwebs and reopen the *boutiques*. In our building,
14 we swept out the squatter who decided to camp in the storage
room for his holiday. People who rarely spoke before August begin
15 conversing like old friends—all asking about vacation—who were
they with, where did they go, and what did they eat.
16

17

18

2   Friday Vendredi   *Week 35*

01

02

03

04

05

06

07

08

09

10

11

12

13

14

15

16

17

18

     I find I advance my French language skills more in September than any other month of the year with these small conversations. The pharmacist remarked that the sea was too cold. The butcher admitted that a month away was too long, that it's nice to be back, and work keeps him in great shape. He flexed his arm for emphasis. He had retired from his own *boucherie*, sold it, then went to work up the street for the other *boucherie* because he missed the workout and his clients. "A man only needs a certain amount of time off," he says. When I asked the fishmonger how he spent his vacation, he winked and said he went fishing. He went on to say he was happy to be gone and glad to be back in equal measure. It seems a long vacation helps one feel ready to return.

5 Monday Lundi   *Week 36*

01 # I am Popular

02 *Rentrée* also means the return of my two beloved market men in
their matching yellow pantaloons. Look at his shopping bag. Where did
03 he get it? Did a grandkid give it to him? Was it a free promotional
item at a market? Did he laugh and say, "I need to have this." Did
04 he always want to be popular? Is he? I shake my head in disbelief
05 and gratitude for this moment. He and his companion meander down
rue Mouffetard, the older of the two unsteady on his feet.

06

07 I was hovering
around the butcher
08 shop waiting for
Christophe. I had
09 my camera in my
hand and was able
10 to capture this
photo undetected.
11

12 Soon, my popular
market men became
13 an obsession and I
began taking photos
14 of them whenever
they came along.

15

16

17

18

01

02

16   They haven't caught me yet.

17

18

7 Wednesday Mercredi

01 # *Baguettes*

02 Each day I walk up to the *boulangerie* and pic up a *baguette du chef,*
distinguished by its end, the *quignon.* The chef snips the end in two
03 prior to baking, creating a two-pronged crablike claw end. The ovens
pump out fresh batches around breakfast, before lunch, and before
04 dinner so your *baguette* is still relatively warm once it hits your table.
But I don't wait that long. I walk my freshly baked prize over to the
05 lovely Christophe who is roasting chickens a few doors down. I offer
06 him the *baguette.* He yanks off his end of *le quignon* and I yank off
mine, wishbone-style. The crunchy crust gives way to an ivory chewy
07 inside *(la mie).* It's a holy moment. I bid him farewell and head to the
fromagerie to choose a soft cheese to accompany the *baguette.* And
08 the French do this every single day!

09

10

11

12

13

14

15

16

17

18

ST. ADRIEN DAY

8 Thursday Jeudi

01   A *baguette* in France must, by law, have only four ingredients:
water, salt, flour, and yeast. You would think they all taste exactly

02 the same. Not so! There is the heat of the oven to consider, the
time the dough is given to rise, and of course, the mood of the

03 baker. Awards are bestowed annually to the bakers who master

04 the art of all three. In my due diligence, I have hopscotched
across Paris to taste the winning *baguettes*. They were all good,

05 *bien sûr,* but not astoundingly better than the award-less *baguette*
I buy every day at lunch. So I had to add other factors to the

06 hunt: Location, charm, and a nearby gurgling fountain all earned

07 bonus points. As the weather cooled, I noted that *baguettes* tasted
better. Furthermore, the taste improved when I could sit outside

08 the bakery with a friend and partake in an impromptu picnic with
said *baguettes* balanced on our laps, and us

09 speckling our shirts with crumbs.

10 I can't say I've come
up with a clear winner.

11 I'm still taste testing.
Oval, round, braided,

12 dense, light, brown,

13 beige . . .

14 *Miam-miam.*

15

16

17

18

MAISON KAYSER

BOULANGERIE PATISSERIE

KAYSER

RUE
DES
CHARTREUX

ST. ALAIN DAY

9 Friday Vendredi   *Week 36*

01   The *boulangerie* doesn't make much money on *baguette* sales.
The prices are fixed by the government. But *boulangeries* sell other
02   worthy loafs to boost the bottom line. Poilâne offers a nice loaf with
its signature "P." There are no preservatives in the bread, which
03   means it's rock hard the next day. The French never throw out
04   bread, hence the culinary inventions of croutons and *pain perdu* or
in English, French toast. The literal translation is "lost bread," the
05   bread you didn't finish the day before. I find the leftover bread
from Poilâne in French toast form the next day to be *fantastique.*
06

07

08

09

10

11

12

13

14

15

16

17

18

Poilâne, 8, rue du Cherche-Midi, 75006

ST. APOLLINAIRE DAY

12 Monday Lundi   *Week 37*

01 The French don't throw out books either. When you visit their
apartments, you'll find bookshelves of yellowed and tattered
02 classics, some likely read during school, all still on display.

03   In France, no bookseller, including Amazon, can discount a book
more than 5 percent. With such a small savings, people prefer
04 shopping in bookstores. Why buy online and miss out on the latest
local gossip from the bookseller?
05

06   Along the Seine, are bookstalls selling vintage tomes. In order
to qualify, you must hold a librarian's degree or related degree.
07 The amount of souvenirs you can sell is also limited. The city wants
the bookstalls to remain as bookstalls, even if most of the money
08 might be made on trinkets.

09

10

11

12

13

14

15

16

17

18

ST. AIMÉ DAY

13 Tuesday Mardi   *Week 37*

Michel de Montaigne

On this day in 1592, Montaigne died. He was known for legitimizing the essay as a form of literature. His essays are some of the most influential ever written. But what I like most about him is his shoe. In India, people rub the truck of Ganesh, the half-man, half-elephant Hindu deity for good luck. In Rome, people rub the foot of St. Peter. But in France, they rub the shoe of a writer.

56, rue des Écoles in square Paul-Painlevé

CROIX GLORIEUSE FEAST DAY

14 Wednesday Mercredi   *Week 37*

01 ## Pigeons of Pompidou

02 As I sat outside the Pompidou modern art museum, thousands of
pigeons descended for a minute, then flew down a nearby street.
03 All day long they fly back and forth. For me, they were a delight
to observe. Perhaps not so for the monsieur.

04

05

06

07

08

09

10

11

12

13

14

15

16

17

18

15 Thursday Jeudi   *Week 37*

01 When I followed the pigeons, they took me down a street with
02 the most marvelous old sign. It was no longer a *boutique* selling bread,
wine, or cheese as the sign indicated. It was a hat shop now. That's
03 how it is in Paris. If the sign is cute, they leave it up, open their
new shop, and get busy making hats. Beauty reigns in Paris.
04

05

06

07

08

09

10

11

12

13

14

15

16

17

18

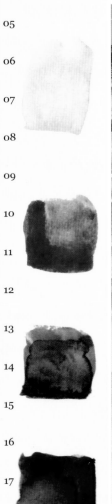

16 Friday Vendredi

01

The Pompidou

02
03
04
05
06

The Pompidou museum was named after Georges Pompidou who was known both as a president of France and instigator of ugly modern architecture in Paris. Whenever you see a modern building in the 13th arrondissement or gaze out over the monstrous Montparnasse tower, you can blame Pompidou. The museum, however, is marvelous. On the day I was there, the guards were sticklers about the No Photos rule, but I managed to sneak one in of this vintage phone. It has a certain *je ne sais quoi* appeal, and a great view of Paris.

07

08

09

10

11

12

13

14

15

16

17

18

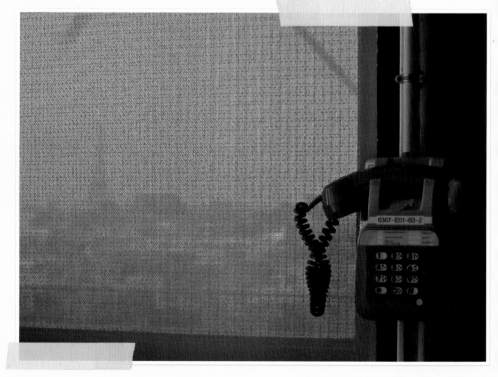

place Georges-Pompidou, 75004

ST. EMILIE DAY

19 Monday Lundi

01

02

"The artist is nothing without the gift, but the gift is nothing without work."

—Émile Zola

03

04

05

06

07

08

09

10

11

12

13

14

15

16

If January has a winter blue hue and May is bright green, September is most definitely olive green. The leaves are on the cusp of calling it quits. They've given the last green they've got, and are heading into a slight fade that will soon turn amber and orange.

17

18

ST.DAVY DAY

20 Tuesday Mardi   *Week 38*

01 The cool snap last night has provoked change. We've pulled out the
coats again. Ivy is always the first to turn toward autumn.

02

03

04

05

06

07

08

09

10

11

12

13

14

15

16

17

18

ST. MATTHIEU DAY

21 Wednesday Mercredi   *Week 38*

01

Secret Paris

02 Paris is filled with secret spaces for those who want respite from
03 the hectic go-go-go of life in a modern city. One of the best
secret spaces is on the rooftop of Galeries Lafayette department
04 store. It's a special place above the hustle-bustle of the street.
After you enter the building, take the escalator to the top . . . so
05 many stories, I lost count. There, you'll find a plain set of stairs.
So plain, in fact, that tourists turn back, assuming the stairs lead
06 to a restricted area. Genius! Take the stairs. They lead to the
07 rooftop where you'll find a *faux* green grass carpet, lounge chairs,
locals resting, and a million-dollar view of ALL the great monuments.

08

09

10

11

12

13

14

15

16

17

18

22 Thursday Jeudi

Week 38

01

02

03

04

05

06

07

08

09

10

11

12

13

14   You'll also find office workers munching salads in their suits,

weary bag-laden marathon shoppers, and people like me who sit

15   quietly for hours sketching, taking photos, and counting their lucky

16   stars to know of such a place.

17

18

40, boulevard Haussmann, 75009

23 Friday Vendredi   *Week 38*

01
The Phantom of the Opera

02 On this day in 1909, *Le Fantôme de l'Opéra* was published as
a serial in a French newspaper. The author, Gaston Leroux, a
03 French journalist, became fascinated with the Paris Opera House
after he covered the news report of a patron who died when
04 struck by a falling chandelier. He knew the building sat atop
catacombs and jail cells, and when a skeleton was discovered in
05 the cellars, inspiration struck. His beauty-and-the-beast tale was
published as a book in 1910. A century later, Disney came out
06 with *Beauty and the Beast* and named the villain Gaston. Leroux
maintained throughout his life that the opera ghost was real.
07

08

09

10

11

12

13

14

15

16

17

18

26 Monday Lundi

01
Ghosts of Luxembourg

02
The Paris park chair may be the most uncomfortable chair in the world to provide the most gratifying experience. The metal cuts into

03
the leg, the armrest seems to be designed for someone larger than the average person, and because of their heft, when dragged across

04
gravel, they create their own unique grating rumble. Yet when the feet are aching or the mind is full, these chairs seem to heal what's

05
ailing. You'll notice how chairs are left as arranged by their last

06
occupants—five in a circle hints at a group, three in a triangle was likely a couple who had a picnic and used the third chair as a table,

07
and two facing each other means one person used the second chair as a footstool. It's the best way to get comfortable enough to sit for

08
an extended period to rest the weary feet and watch the scene.

09

10

11

12

13

14

15

16

17

18

15, rue de Vaugirard, 75006

27 Tuesday Mardi

Week 39

01

Vincent Van Gogh

02 This artist of Post-Impressionism once said, "To do good work, one must eat well, be well housed, have one's fling from time to time, 03 smoke one's pipe, and drink one's coffee in peace."

04 You'll find his work at Musée d'Orsay but 05 his ghost is at a *café* drinking his coffee 06 in peace.

07

08

09

10

11

12

13

14

15

16

17

18

ST. VENCELAS DAY

28 Wednesday Mercredi

01 I took off for the café in Jardin du Luxembourg today for front row seats to nature's most brazen costume change. I sat outside

02 under the awning when it began to lightly rain. Just then a breeze turned up and thousands of leaves began to fall. It was the most

03 glorious symphony of leaves, rain, and wind. An older gentleman

04 noticed, too. He promptly took a seat nearby, grabbed an abandoned copy of Le Monde and started reading.

15 Just then a loud racket of DANCE MUSIC erupted from inside the café. Instant rage! I rose from my seat, walked to the

16 open door, glared at the waiter within, and closed it firmly with

17 an audible huff. Monsieur Le Monde looked up from his paper and nodded. I have never felt so French, so old, or so cool as I did in

18 that glorious moment in the rain.

29 Thursday Jeudi

01

02

03

0

05

06

07

08

09

10 On the beat in Jardin du Luxembourg. Looking for trouble.
Finding giggles instead.

11

14

15

16

17

18

ST. JÉRÔME DAY

01

Autumn left me breathless. My eyes opened. The leaves, once

02 an invisible backdrop, turned to flowers.

03

04

05

06

07

08

09

10

11

12

13

14

15

16

17

18

ST. GÉRARD DAY

3 Monday Lundi

01

02

03

04

05

06

07

08

09

10

11

Allan Kardec's Birthday

12

13 Allan Kardec was born today in 1804 and was known for developing "Spiritism," the art of talking to the dead. He conducted séances, which were popular at the time. His *nom de plume* was Hippolyte Léon Denizard Rivail. Paris has a long history, so there are likely plenty of ghosts walking around and observing the buffoonery that is humanity. What I like about Kardec is that his "Spiritism" justifies my friendship with the ghostly Hemingway.

14

15

16

17 "When good Americans die, they go to Paris."
—Oscar Wilde, *The Picture of Dorian Gray*

18

ST. FRANÇOIS D'ASSISE DAY

4 Tuesday Mardi

Week 40

01

Autumn in Paris is a mix of somber and sunshine.

02

03

04

05

06

07

08

09

10

11

12

13

14

15

16

17

18

5 Wednesday Mercredi   *Week 40*

01
02
03
04
05
06
07
08
09
10
11
12
13
14
15
16
17
18

ST. BRUNO DAY

6 Thursday Jeudi

Week 40

01

02

03

04

05

06

07

09

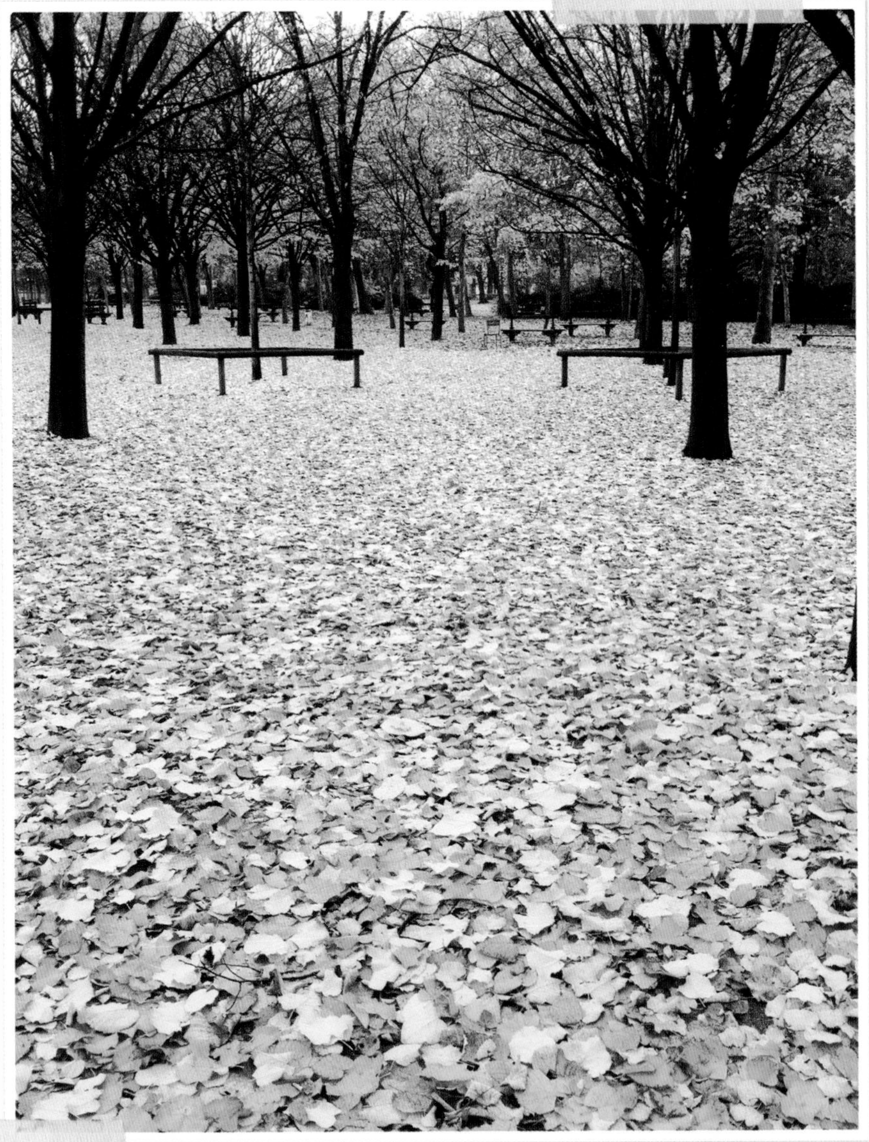

11

12

13

14

15

16

17

18

7 Friday Vendredi

01

The leaves fell perfectly when I strolled by. The next day a gust of wind arrived and swooshed them all away.

02

03

04

05

06

07

08

09

10

11

12

13

14

15

16

17

18

Medici Fountain, Jardin du Luxembourg, 75006

203

10 Monday Lundi

Week 41

01

02

"Life starts all over again when it gets crisp in the fall."

—F. S. Fitzgerald

03

04

05

06

07

08

09

10

11

12

13

14

15

16

17

18

11 Tuesday Mardi   *Week 41*

01 The preferred season for every Parisian is autumn. Sure, spring
has blooming trees and summer has a certain sizzle (winter
02 doesn't even make the shortlist), but autumn trumps them
all. First off, the tourists have been thinned out so museums
03 cease to be an exercise in patience and tolerance. Then, as the
weather cools, there is a reintroduction of red wine to the
04 table, not that it left exactly, but in warmer seasons there is
often the dilemma between red, white, and rosé. With the
05 leaf changing, the city is back to the
assumption that it will be red for
06
the evening and everyone can
07 get back to making other
important decisions, like
08 which cheese should accompany
said red.
09

10

11

12

13

14

But the best part of autumn is
15 the fashion. Women go positively batty
for the latest boots, and if you have
16 a particularly stunning trench you will be
asked where you bought it by fashion-
17 obsessed strangers on the street. There
is nothing like the approval of a Parisian lady.
18

12 Wednesday Mercredi

01

02

03

04

05

06

07

08

09

10

11

12

13

14

15

16

17

"I firmly believe that with the right footwear, one can rule the world."

—Bette Midler

18

13 Thursday Jeudi

Week 41

01 "It is now the fall of my second year in Paris. I was sent
here for a reason I have not yet been able to fathom. I have
02 no money, no resources, no hopes. I am the happiest man alive.
A year ago, six months ago, I thought I was an artist. I no longer
03 think about it. I am."

04 —Henry Miller

05

06

07

08

09

10

11

12

13

14

15

16

17

18

14 Friday Vendredi

01 This weekend marks the birthday of Oscar Wilde, the famed outrageous writer of witticisms. I say his birthday is this weekend
02 because the plaque on the apartment where he died states he was born October 15, 1856, but his grave in Père Lachaise states
03 he was born October 16, 1856. It's not like the French to make errors in history and stone. No one seems quick to change one or
04 the other, so I'll just chalk it up to one of those quirky Paris facts.

05

06

07

08

09

10

11

12

13

14

15 He died in the Hôtel d'Alsace at 13, rue des Beaux Arts, 75006. As he lay dying, he remarked, "I am dying beyond my
16 means."

17 It was Wilde who inspired me to take my journal with me wherever I go. "I never travel without my diary," he said. "One
18 should always have something sensational to read in the train."

17 Monday Lundi   *Week 42*

01 ## Paris Artists

02 Along with my journal, I also take my camera with me wherever I
go because one never knows when a lovely moment will reveal itself.
03 Paris is kind to those who appreciate her lines. I can walk down
the same street a hundred times and not see anything exciting, then
04 the sun shines down at a particular angle and what was once mundane
turns to gold.
05

06

07

08

09

10

11

12

13

14

15

16   And of course, I can be there to capture it because the best
way to be a good photographer is to embrace the number one rule of
17 photography: The best camera you have is the one you have with you.

18

01   If there is
02 something remotely wrong with your
03 camera, you'll leave it at home. Here in
04 the land of tourists,
05 I see it all the time. Someone brings
06 their fancy camera out on their first
07 day on the town,
08 but because it's too heavy or complicated
09 or whatever, they leave it in the hotel
10 room the next day and opt to take
11 photos with their
12 phones so they can easily and effectively
13 polish up the reputation of their
14 shiny social media
15 selves. The new camera sits silent
16 and sullen in the hotel room watching
17 the maid make
18 the bed.

ST.RENÉ DAY

01
02
03
04

The path of the artist is littered with unused art supplies. In my wake, I have left reams of paper, pens, paints, stamps, and even cameras. Some were too complicated, too goopy, too thick, too thin, too hard or soft. But in time, I learned what I needed and what I didn't. If I had to leave all my art supplies behind today, I would happily walk away with a small watercolor set, two small paint brushes, and of course, my small camera.

05
06
07
08
09
10
11
12
13
14
15
16
17
18

ST. ADELINE DAY

01   When buying a camera, I buy the smallest camera with the
best lens. And then add a heaping dollop of patience. There is
02   nothing quite like a new camera to knock your confidence down a
few notches. For the first week with my new camera, I played
03   with all the fancy buttons and wheels, snapping terrible shot after
terrible shot. Frustrated, in the second week I resorted to the
04   Auto feature, which took much better photos than I could.

05

06

07

08

09

10

11

12

13

14

15

16
Sometimes it's just about noticing when interesting foregrounds
17   walk in front of interesting backgrounds. Like how this person's
clothing matches the bike, right down to the ribbon on the hat.

18

21 Friday Vendredi

01 I went over to Jardin du Luxembourg once again to capture as
much of autumn as I could with my camera and watercolor set. It
02 seems autumn changes most dramatically in this park from week to
week, so frequent visits are fruitful. Usually the groundskeepers
03 sweep up and wipe down every bench, chair, and inch of grass in
this park. It always seems pristine. The one exception is autumn.
04 They let the leaves fall and blanket the park, allowing us all to
05 admire autumn in all its hues. Then the most polite thing happens.

16 Rather than scooping up the leaves with a machine or loudly
17 blowing them into a pile, disturbing the peace of strollers like me,
they quietly rake them up. Swish swish swish until the final leaf
18 has been gathered.

24 Monday Lundi

01

02

03

04

05

06

07

08

09

10

11

12

13

14

15

16

17

18

Twenty Queens of France

Jardin du Luxembourg has a collection of twenty statues, each representing a queen of France.

A few notable queens standing guard in the garden:

Anne of France was one of the most powerful women in the late fifteenth century and was called Madame la Grande. The Great Lady. Another queen, Anne Marie Louise d'Orléans was known as La Grande Mademoiselle. She wanted to marry for love. When her parents wouldn't approve, she opted to not marry at all. Bertha of Burgundy also wanted to marry someone who wasn't preapproved. In her case it was her cousin because they were too closely related. No one wants a Hapsburg chin situation.

01 Bertha was the daughter of Conrad the Peaceful, and Valentina
02 Visconti was the daughter of John II the Good. Anne of Brittany
      joined Brittany to France. Brittany butter cookies, *galettes*
03 *bretonnes*, are from here. Thanks, Anne. Margaret of Provence was
      the wife of Louix IX. What's most fascinating about her was her
04 family. Her three younger sisters became the Queen of England,
      Queen of Germany, and Queen of Sicily. And we can thank Marie
05 de' Medici for giving us the grand Jardin du Luxembourg where we
06 can mix and mingle with the who-was-who of French royalty.

07

08

09

10

11

12

13

14

15

16

17

18

The Statue of Liberty was no queen but you can find her replica in the garden.

26 Wednesday Mercredi

01 # Alimentation Générale

02 The Alimentation Générale is a chain of little markets found all over
Paris. They are useful for a midnight snack, say, if your houseguests
03 from across the pond request chips and dip. The proprietors usually
wear a green smock. These little markets were made famous in the
04 film *Amélie* where she befriends the boy who works at the market
05 in Montmartre. That particular store can be found at 56, rue des
Trois Frères, 75018.

06

07

08

09

10

11

12

13

14

15

16

17

18

ST. EMELINE DAY

27 Thursday Jeudi

01   In October, the markets are full of fruits and vegetables. October is the one time of the year when summer crops of

02 crimson tomatoes mingle with the autumn crops of otherworldly mushrooms, which mingle with the citrus fruit imported for

03 winter.

04   Up my street, there is a grocer who makes little pyramids of his fruit. He seems bored and miserable. I much prefer the

05 grocer at the bottom of the street who spills out the fruit in a

06 veritable cornucopia of celebration and abundance. He's always got a smile on his face.

07

08

09

10

11

12

13

14

15

16

17

18

28 Friday Vendredi

01

02

03

04

05

06

07

08

09

10

11

12

13

14

15

16

17

18

Some of these little markets are also affiliated with package delivery services. So at times, I'll receive a notice in my mailbox or on my door that my package has been delivered to a particular grocery store. I've also discovered packages to be delivered to local eyeglass *boutiques* and chocolate shops. I suppose it's a way to get more foot traffic in your door. At first I found it odd to walk into my local market with a tracking slip, but my package was there, handed across the counter with a friendly smile.

With the autumn leaves, ripe squash, and bright citrus, there is no question that the dominant hue for October is orange.

31 Monday Lundi

01

Then the last of the leaves fell. We gathered our scarves closer
to our necks, zipped up our coats, and braced ourselves for winter.

02

03

04

05

06

07

08

09

10

11

12

13

14

15

16

17

18

place Louis Aragon, 47, quai de Bourbon, Île Saint-Louis, 75004

TOUSSAINT/ALL SAINTS DAY

1 Tuesday Mardi

Week 44

01
02
03
04
05
06
07
08
09
10
11
12
13
14
15
16
17
18

The days are noticeably shorter now. The lamps flicker on in late afternoon and the city takes on a gloomy glow. Of course, this glow at other times of the year is revered, but in November, it means one thing: We are descending into the dark season. With the trees now bare of leaves, architectural details reveal themselves. A nice, but small benefit to an otherwise bleak time.

DÉFUNTS / ALL SOULS DAY

2 Wednesday Mercredi

01

After the first cold snap, the streets are bare. Everyone huddles
02 inside for a few days, but after accepting the new normal of
gloves and thick scarves, we venture out again, reclaiming our
03 local *bistros* as an extension of home.

04

05

06

07

08

09

10

11

12

13

14

15   The menus have changed with the season. *Cassoulet, raclette,*
and *fondue* are the specials of the day and our spirits are lifted.
16 Pair dinner with a deep red from Saint-Émilion and you've got
yourself a feast. If you're going to hibernate for the season, Paris
17 is where you want to be.

18

3 Thursday Jeudi

01

City of Light

02 Some say Paris got it's nickname because of it's enlightened thinking
in terms of culture and learning. The French translation of City of
03 Light is *Ville Lumière*, meaning "city of enlightenment." Others argue
that it's because of its early adoption of street lighting.
04

05

06

07

08

09

10

11

12

13

14

15 The city "turned on the switch" in a major way during the
Exposition Universelle of 1900, the world's fair hosted by Paris.
The fair celebrated the achievements of the past century and
16 showcased new developments for the future. The Palace of
Electricity was illuminated with over five thousand lights and
17 wowed the world. Soon after, major cities of the world adopted
citywide electric lighting.
18

ST. CHARLES DAY

4 Friday Vendredi

Week 44

01

02

03

04

05

06

07

08

09

10

11

12

13

14

15

16

17

18

7 Monday Lundi

01
Marie Curie's Birthday

02 Today in 1867, the scientist who would would change the course
of medicine was born. Her name was Marie Skłodowska but most
03 know her as Marie Curie.

04   "All I want is a postcard of Marie Curie."

05   This was the request of one Polish relative that arrived in
Paris for the weekend. Usually the requests are simple: Eiffel
06 Tower, picnic in the park, that crowd-pleaser the *Mona Lisa*. But
after all my time wandering around Paris, I had yet to come across
07 a postcard of Marie Curie. In short, she was a Polish woman who
came to France to study physics and chemistry, as she could not
08 in Poland. She married Pierre Curie and they spent their lives
09 hovered over microscopes and test tubes. *Quelle romantique!*

10

18
Musée Curie, 1, rue Pierre et Marie Curie, 75005

01 # Marie Curie Cheat Sheet

02 * Discovered radium and polonium (named after Poland)

03 * Pioneered research in radioactivity

* First woman to win the Nobel Prize

04 * First woman to win two Nobel Prizes, in both physics and chemistry

05 * First woman to receive a Ph.D. from a French university

06 * First female professor at the Sorbonne

* Established the field of radiation therapy for cancer

07 * Her research made medical use of X-rays possible

08 * With prolonged exposure
to radium, she developed
09 leukemia and died
10 in 1934

* She was buried at the
11 Pantheon alongside other
12 great thinkers

* After death, the
13 Musée Curie was opened
14 on the ground floor in
her laboratory
15 * Inside said museum, one
16 can purchase postcards
17 of Marie Curie

18 Thank goodness.

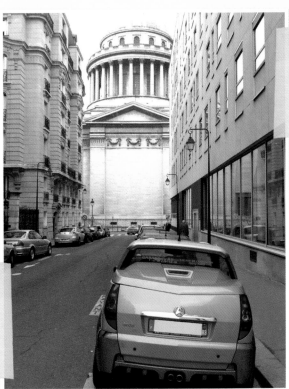

place du Panthéon, 75005

ST. THÉODORE DAY

9 Wednesday Mercredi

01 A Marie Curie postcard hunt request is pure pleasure compared
to the Arc de Triomphe request. There is always that one
02 tourist who comes to town and insists on eating a crêpe in the
shadow of the Arc de Triomphe. Locals hesitate to indulge this
03 request as they know the reality is vastly different from the
rosy soft fantasy. Our tourist wants the calm boulevard, shaded
04 with trees. They want to watch people strolling by. They want
to bask in the sunshine. They want the quaint café with the
05 waiter who speaks English with a French accent. These tourists
never assume the waiter speaks French. Always English
06 with a charming accent. The reality is the incessant
groan of traffic, screaming, and honking. There is
07 shuffling through hoards of tourists who waddle by,
complaining about blisters and aching feet.
08

09

10

11

13

14

15

16

17

18

10 Thursday Jeudi

01

02

03   The crêpes are even overpriced in euros. To convert
04   currency in your head would send you into a tailspin of regret.
     But our stubborn tourist will not be swayed, so off you go. As you
     sit squished into a *terrasse* seat, you gaze off over the crowds
05   to the Arc de Triomphe. It really is an impressive war memorial.
     Then you smile and realize that the scene is perfect and
06   appropriate. A different, but much preferred, kind of war.

07

Once fortified
on the world's
priciest pancake,
you can walk
halfway across the
boulevard to the
light and pretend
to be hitchhiking
along the world's
most chaotic
intersection. Then
take the tunnel
beneath the road
to see the Arc de
Triomphe up close.

11 Friday Vendredi

01

02

Arc de Triomphe
Fast Facts

03

04

05

06 * Built by Napoléon for his army

* He and his army had conquered much of Europe by then and

07 were considered invincible

08 * Napoléon promised his army they would return home through
its arches

09 * The arch is meant to celebrate victories and has its victories

10 carved in its walls

* Names of generals are also carved in the walls. Those with

11 underlined names show that the general died in battle

12 * Germans marched under the arch during the Franco-Prussian War

* The Nazis did the same in World War II

13 * Napoléon died before construction was complete, but his body was

14 marched through the arches on its way to its final resting place at

15 the Military Museum

* On November 11, 1923, the memorial flame at the base of the

16 arch was lit and is rekindled every night at dusk to honor the

17 unknown soldier

18

14 Monday Lundi

13

Yesterday was the anniversary of the Paris Attacks of 2015.

14

15

16

"My dear, In the midst of hate, I found there was, within me, an invincible love. In the midst of tears, I found there was, within me, an invincible smile. In the midst of chaos, I found there was, within me, an invincible calm. I realized, through it all, that . . . In the midst of winter, I found there was, within me, an invincible summer. And that makes me happy. For it says that no matter how hard the world pushes against me, within me, there's something stronger—something better, pushing right back."

17

18

—Albert Camus

ST.ALBERT DAY

01 I met friends for drinks and dinners. We huddled together, heads bent together softly conversing. They told their story of that night.
02 Offloading trauma. When something happens and we replay it in our mind over and over, that's trauma. The best way to yank it out of
03 the psyche is to talk about it. So I sat and listened. Then we moved on to other subjects, then we veered back. Then off again. Then on
04 again. And that's how it goes until you forget to talk about it.
05

06
07
08
09
10
11
12
13
14
15
16
17
18

16 Wednesday Mercredi   *Week 46*

01
Destruction des Animaux Nuisibles

02 Speaking of vermin . . . this place, featured in the film *Ratatouille*,
really exists. They cater to the shaken homesteader who has been
03 forced into studying the fine art of obliterating creepy crawlies.
04 The shop has been in business since 1872. The shop name is
easy enough to translate. And it carries all manner of potions and
05 contraptions to take care of the nastiest of houseguests.

06

07

08

09

10

11

12

13

14

15   The mice in my building usually stay out of sight during the day,
16 but often I can hear them scrambling, scratching, and searching
behind the walls, haunting me like in "The Tell-Tale Heart."

17   "I became insane, with long intervals of horrible sanity."
—Edgar Allan Poe

18
8, rue des Halles, 75001

231

ST. ELISABETH DAY

17 Thursday Jeudi

Week 46

01 ## Beaujolais Nouveau Day

02 Today is the celebration of the first wine harvested
from this year's crop. Unlike most wines that should
03 age, Beaujolais nouveau is meant to be consumed
immediately. There is a race to carry the first
04 bottles to Paris. Bistros and bars hang signs and
05 balloons *"Le Beaujolais nouveau est arrivé !"*

06

07

08

09

10

11

12

13

14

15

16

17

18

104, rue Mouffetard,
75005

ST. AUDE DAY

18 Friday Vendredi

01
02
03
04
05
06
07
08
09
10
11
12
13
14
15
16
17
18

Never one to miss out on a big day of celebrating wine, the friends and I sidle up to a bar to partake in this annual festival. Truth be told, we are not fans. It's a rather young wine, and even my unsophisticated palate can hardly handle this swill. But after we finish our first glass, we order what we really want, and that's the best part of this event.

21 Monday Lundi   *Week 47*

01 The city is plunged in darkness by 4:30 each day. These are
definitely the longest nights of the year. If one had to choose a
02 hue for late afternoon in November, it would be black and white.

03
- TATIN DE TOMATE, courgette et oignon.
- CAPPUCCINO de potimarron aux langoustines, chantilly aux épices.
- MOELLEUX mozzarella, chorizo et épinard.
- TERRINE DE CHEVREUIL et jambon Serrano.
- LINGUINE au aubergine, tomate cerise, mozzarella DI-BUFALA et basilic.
- JOUE DE BOEUF BRAISÉ, purée de pomme de terre et flan de carottes.
- CIVET DE CHEVREUIL, pomme vapeur et petit légumes. 16
- FILET DE ROUGET, risotto crémeux et légumes du soleil. 18

- CLAFOUTIS DE REINE CLAUDE. 6€
- PAIN PERDU aux figues et son sorbet. 6€
- TIRAMISU à la confiture de lait. 7€
- MI-CUIT AU CHOCOLAT, passion et sorbet citron vert.

22 Tuesday Mardi

01
02
03

There are times when you look at a menu and realize you can understand everything. Your French lessons are coming along. You pat yourself on the back. Then you realize the menu is in English and you're back to low self-esteem in the languages department.

04
05
06
07
08
09
10
11
12
13
14
15
16
17
18

salmon club sandwich

RE & CARPACCIO

tartare, asian flavour

b's tartare, french fries and green salad

beef tartare, french fries and green salad

Italian Tartar

ERS

burger, french fries

burger (mozzarella, roquette salad, tomato)

burger

cheeseburger

ian burger

cheeseburger, french fries

breast with risotto and mushrooms

ccata pasta gratin with parmesan

with foie gras and duck fillet

entrecôte 280gr with french fries

of beef, pepper sauce and green beans

tuna steak. half baked sauce vierge

cooked skin side

23 Wednesday Mercredi

01 The French are the first to admit their handwriting is "terribleeh."
They say it's because they were never taught to print in school.
02 They only learned to write. I'm not sure they learned that either.

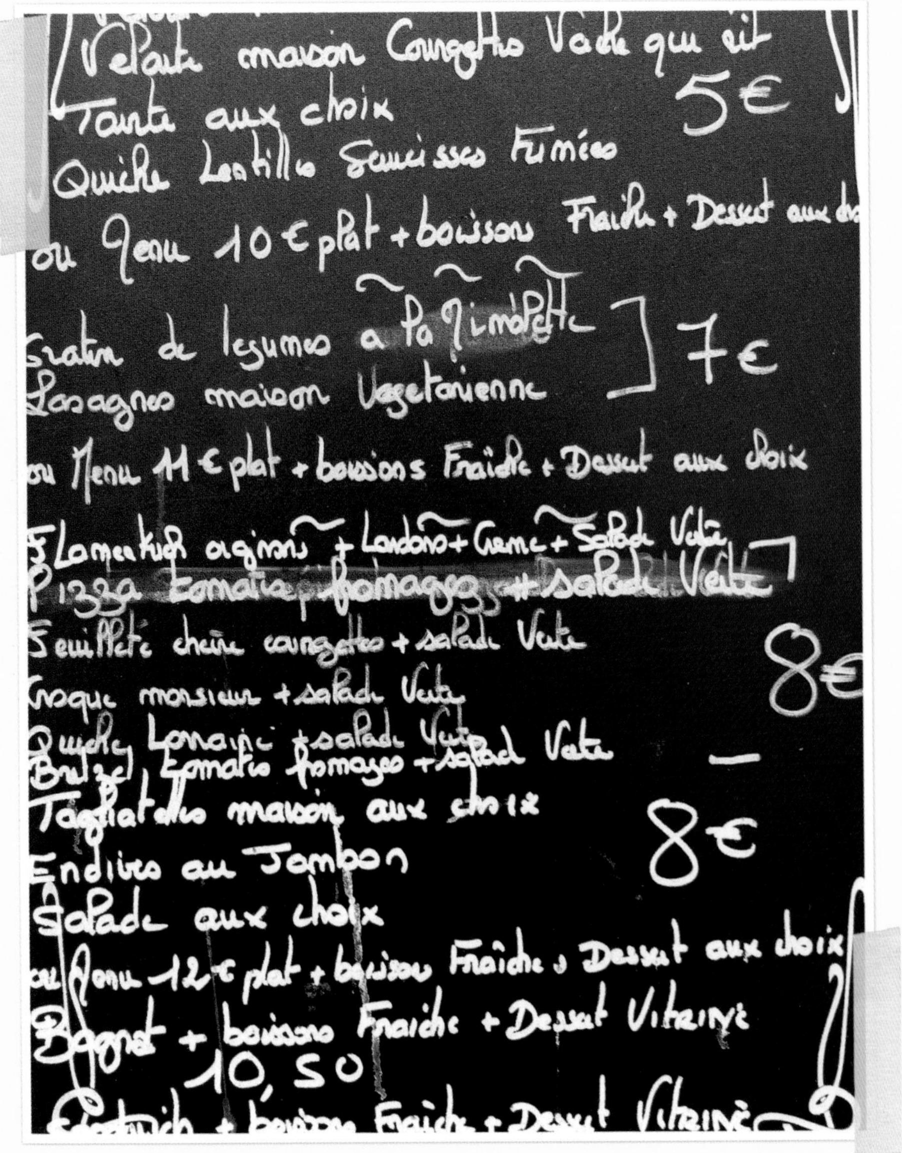

03

04

05

06

07

08

09

10

11

12

13

14

15

16

17

18

24 Thursday Jeudi   *Week 47*

Typique French Ladies

It's hard to nail down a typical French style when we have so many variations walking the streets of Paris. Both these French ladies are out shopping. They will both arrive home with a warm *baguette* in their possession. They will both have a glass of wine as they prepare dinner. And they'll both likely watch the news. So even though they appear quite different, they are indeed, rather similar.

01
02
03
04
05
06
07
08
09
10
11
12
13
14
15
16
17
18

ST. CATHERINE DAY

25 Friday Vendredi

01 When I was a kid, I dreamed of having a spiral staircase. A spiral

adds elegance and whimsy to a house. When I arrived in Paris, I

02 soon realized I had been given an entire city of spiral staircases.

With space at a minimum, spiral is the way to go in Paris. Stairs

03 are yet another secret to longevity for Parisians.

04

05

06

07

08

09

10

11

12

13

14

15

16

17

18

ST. JACQUES DAY

28 Monday Lundi

01 There isn't much sun at all, even at high noon. The days are muted, beige, and winter blue. It's not depressing. Save that for February.

02 In November, the somber hues are poetic. If you were to opt for poetic brooding, November in Paris would be the month for you. The

03 French are a morose lot, so November fits their mood perfectly.

04

05

06

07

08

09

10

11

12

13

14

15

16

17

18

29 Tuesday Mardi   *Week 48*

01 Everyone stays in on the first night of a cold spell. We aren't
    ready for winter. We've become shy to the elements. *Bistros*
02 are empty and sad, having planned for a party that didn't happen.
    On my evening in from the cold, I watched the French version
03 of *Family Feud*. The question was, "What would you do in winter
    that you would never do in summer?" The top response was "Ski."
04 Fair enough. That makes sense. The second response was "Serve
05 *fondue*." Evidently you would NEVER serve *fondue* in other
    seasons. It would be impolite. It would be downright *gauche*. It's only
06 for winter. That seemed like enough information to get me out the
07 door. We emerged from our tiny apartment and ventured forth for

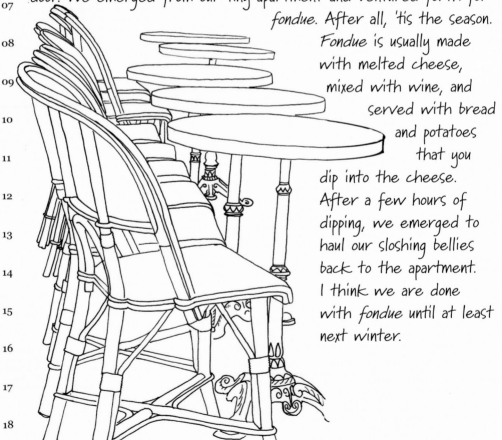

fondue. After all, 'tis the season.
Fondue is usually made
with melted cheese,
mixed with wine, and
served with bread
and potatoes
that you
dip into the cheese.
After a few hours of
dipping, we emerged to
haul our sloshing bellies
back to the apartment.
I think we are done
with *fondue* until at least
next winter.

08
09
10
11
12
13
14
15
16
17
18

ST. ANDRÉ DAY

01
02
03
04
05
06
07
08
09
10
11
12
13
14
15
16
17
18

"France has the only two things toward which we drift
as we grow older—intelligence and good manners."
—F. S. Fitzgerald

ST. FLORENCE DAY

1 Thursday Jeudi   *Week 48*

01 # Christmas Markets

02 December in Paris is enchanting. Christmas markets have popped up
all over the city, offering everything from hot chocolate to glass-

03 blown ornaments. The twinkle lights have appeared almost over night.

04 On brisk evenings, I take long walks and watch the azure sky fade
to black as the twinkling begins. Some streets create a canopy of

05 lights cascading down, luring shoppers to the *boutiques.*

06

07

08

09

10

11

12

13

14

15

16

17

18

2 Friday Vendredi

01 I don't quite understand the ornaments
in Paris. Sure there is the *typique*
02 Nutcracker soldier and ballerina, which
are definitely Noël-esque, but then
03 they have other ornaments that
have a vague tie-in to the holiday.
04

05   They go mad for carp
and love to dangle this fish
06 from the branches of
les sapins. Is it a whole
07 "Jesus fed the village
with fish" thing? Is it
08 an obscure reference
to Christmas dinner?
09 Though usually lamb or
goose is the main protein
10 of the day. Or do they
simply like how fish
11 scales shimmer in
the light?
12

13   *Qui sait?*

14

15

16

17

18

5 Monday Lundi

01

Père Noël?

02

03

04

05

06

07

08

09

10

11

12

13   Santa is springing up everywhere. Today I found him at 2, rue
des Petits-Pères. Two of these bearded beauties flank the doors
14   of the main entrance to this building, which was once a convent,
then after the French Revolution when convents were abolished,
15   it became a town hall. Eventually it was turned into barracks,
then a bank. Now it's office space. All the while having our two
16   little pères watching and waiting to see what comes next.

17

18

6 Tuesday Mardi

01

Saint Nicolas?

02

03

04

05

06

07

08

09

10

11

12

13 After a year of running, by December I've usually hit a wall of
fatigue. Though my mind is still going, my body feels like a lazy git.
14 So when I spotted Santa taking in the rare winter sun and sipping
legal addictive stimulants, I knew I had to figure out a way to find
15 harmony between my productive self and my lazy self. I mean, it's
December and Santa is in his peak period, yet he found time to
16 sit at a café and soak in a few rays of sunshine. Or maybe he's
out for a rare coffee to celebrate his name day.
17

18

7 Wednesday Mercredi

01

02

03

The Christmas market on Champs-Élysées

04 has erected skating rink. I sussed it out a few days
ago and decided that it wasn't up to snuff. Too long and

05 narrow, which meant you'd have to slow down on the ends.

06 Plus, there were six-foot flower pots lined down the middle
of the rink for *décor*. Don't the French know that flowerpots

07 get in the way of any whirly-woos you might want to practice in
the middle of the rink? People from northern climates are super

08 snooty about rinks. Don't argue with us. It's a birthright. There's

09 nothing that can be done about it except get your rinks up to snuff
or suffer the silent scorn of northerners everywhere.

10

So when Christophe and I went to the

11 Christmas market and he said he wanted to
go skating, I had plenty of hesitation. I mean,

12 it's not even big enough for a decent Zamboni
cleanup every few hours. Pshaw! I asked

13 Christophe if he knew how to skate.

14 "No, not really. Let's go!"

15 There is always that moment . . . that

16 glorious moment, when you've been with someone
and they don't know just how great you are.

17 I mean, they think you're great and all, but they
don't even know.

18

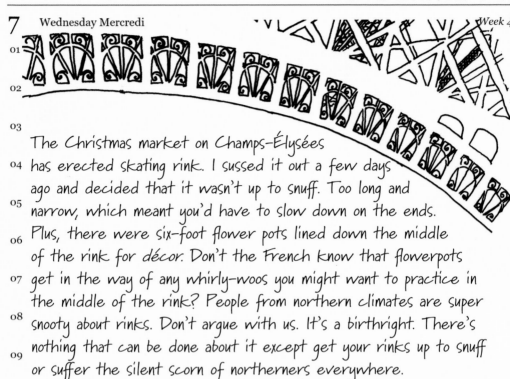

8 Thursday Jeudi

01 So when he stepped onto the ice and
hesitated at the rail, I stepped on next
02 to him and BOLTED. I flew like I had
rockets strapped to the back of my skates.
03 I did a few crosscuts at the end of the
narrow rink, whipped around, flew back,
04 and when I came upon a flowerpot at the
end of the rink, I grabbed it and swung
05 around for another lap. Maybe that's why
the flowerpots are there because I didn't
06 even have to slow down. When I returned
to Christophe, I started talking with him
07 skating backward.
08

09 The only person better than me was
the ref. In fact, if this were the
10 Olympics, I was seriously
in second place after him.
11 We're talking Silver, people.
Bronze goes to a couple
12 from Minnesota because,
well, they have long winters, too.
13 But I won my Silver by a long shot.
14

15 Back home, I can hold my own but
I've got nothing to show off. But here
16 in Paris, put me in skates and I'm a star.

17

18

247

9   Friday Vendredi   *Week 49*

01   # The Crêpe Guy

02   The unsung hand models of Paris. How hypnotizing to watch these

03   guys pouring the batter onto the skillet, smoothing it around with a trowel, and artfully flipping it before adding toppings.

04   The *crêpe* is a quick, fresh, and delicious thin pancake filled with basically anything you would use to fill a sandwich or omelet.

05   You'll find two types of *crêperies* in Paris: the sit-down restaurants and the stand-up street vendors. At the restaurants, they usually

06   serve up this delicate pancake with luxurious fillers like white asparagus and Béarnaise sauce. The street vendors aren't so

07   elegant, but sometimes you just want eggs, mushrooms, and cheese

08   in your *crêpe*, and you want it fast.

09

10

11

12

13

14

15

16

17

18

12 Monday Lundi

01
02
03
04
05

My first memory of Paris was the moment I ate my first crêpe. It was a cold winter day. I was standing on one of those picturesque medieval streets in Saint-Germain-des-Prés in the 6th arrondissement. I went with a Nutella filling. The crêpe was warm. The chocolate sauce had melted in between the folds. It was the most heavenly culinary experience. In that moment I knew I was the luckiest girl in the world.

06
07
08

These days I usually go to the same guy. You get loyal really quickly when one offers a better secret sauce than another. He has a spicy mayo I love and it goes well with the ham and mushrooms. French is his second language, too, so we speak slowly together as steam rises from the skillet.

09
10
11
12
13
14
15
16
17
18

13 Tuesday Mardi   *Week 50*

01   People are beginning to leave for the holidays. This isn't a mass
     exodus like in August. Many people stay in Paris as their families live
02   nearby or are a short train ride away. Still, there is a lot of airport
     action. One of the best tourist attractions is one that most don't
03   even notice: the carry-on baggage measuring stand at the EasyJet
     gate at most European airports. EasyJet is a discount airline and
04   is very strict about their carry-on limit. They charge more if you
05   didn't pay to check your bag online and don't pass the test at the
     measuring stand, thereby having to pay to check your bag at the
06   gate. First, a ticket agent pulls a dozen questionable carry-ons out of
     the line. The rest of us stand in silent relief that our bags weren't
07   chosen. You and your shame are marched over to the stand where
08   you must be able to easily slide your bag into the box, which is the
     exact measurement of the maximum size for carry-ons.

09

10

11

12

13

14

15

16

17

18

14 Wednesday Mercredi   *Week 50*

01   We watch on as our fellow passengers try to jam their bags into
the box. A dozen of Cinderella's stepsisters try in vain to magically
02 shrink down their bags so they fit. No one wants to wait at baggage
claim at the other end. The horror. They can't believe it doesn't fit.

03   The tag stated this was the regulation size for most airlines. Most. Not all.

04 Failure falls down their backs in beads of sweat. As if on cue, we see

05 Cinderella sway by with her carry-on, and surprisingly, her bag is called into

06 question. She nods, smiles, and easily slides her bag into the stand. Clearly,

07 she has done this before and has mastered this moment. The harried

08 dozen stand defeated with baggage claim tickets in hand. They watch her,

09 gobsmacked, and take mental note for next time as she sashays onto the plane.

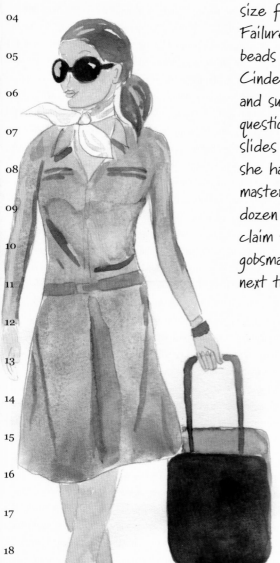

10

11

12

13

14

15

16

17

18

ST. NINON DAY

15 Thursday Jeudi

01

Gustave Eiffel's Birthday

02

03

On this day in 1832, Gustave Eiffel was born. He would go on to create the inner frame of the Statue of Liberty, a railway station and bridge in Budapest, and an obscure little monument in Paris.

04

05

06

07

08

09

10

11

12

13

14

15

16

17

18

16 Friday Vendredi

01

Eiffel Tower Fast Facts

02

03

* Built for the 1889 Paris Universal Exposition. It was going to be dismantled afterward.

04

05

* Thanks to radio, the tower was saved and became a convenient antenna.

06

07

08

* When Hitler visited the tower, someone cut the cables so he would have to climb the 1665 stairs.

09

10

11

* The tower is painted three shades of brown. Dark on the bottom and lighter at the top to give the illusion that it's higher than it is.

12

13

* The paint on the tower weighs the same as ten elephants.

14

* At first, the people of Paris were "against the erection . . . of this useless and monstrous Eiffel Tower."

15

16

* If you stand there long enough on a cloudy day, you can take pictures of cloud animals.

17

18

19 Monday Lundi   *Week 51*

01   It's a challenge to take a unique photo of the world's most
photographed monument. With every visit, I've tried, and then with
02   an online search, discovered that my photos weren't just not unique,
but actually *typique*. *Le sigh*.
03

04   The carousels are back and spinning all over Paris. The city has
thirty-five permanent carousels year-round, and adds another twenty
05   for the season. The Musée des Arts Forains displays a collection
of vintage carousel pieces and other carnival objects, including a
06   carousel powered by the riders who are pedaling. The museum
opens its doors during the Christmas season. Back in the glory days,
07   carousels were painted and repainted to keep their vibrancy. Now
the museum meticulously repairs and restores old pieces.
08

09

10

11

12

13

14

15

16

17

18

01

Le Bon Marché Rive Gauche

02 Gustave Eiffel also redesigned one of Paris' grandest department
stores. Le Bon Marché Rive Gauche is a hotspot of festive fun
03 during December. The *papetière* alone is worth the visit. And when
you get hungry, the marvelous food court, La Grande Épicerie,
04 will entice you with the most splendid display of expertly packaged
goodies. The French are masters of pretty packaging. Each box of
05 cookies and can of candies is like an ornament.

06

07

08

09

10

11

12

13

14

15

16

17

18

255

21 Wednesday Mercredi

01

Vert et Rouge

02
03
04

In a desperate attempt to create a Christmas card, I scoured the city for scenes in green and red. Not easy in Paris. It turns out that the green and red combo is a rarity in the city of lights. I found a few examples, but I quickly concluded that *vert et rouge* are not the hues of Paris in December.

05

06

07

08
09

10

11

12

13

14

15

16

17

18

01

Bleu et Jaune

02

03

04

I should have realized that with all the twinkle lights in the city and the late afternoon sunset, the tone of the season is a cool azure blue from the sky and the bright yellows of the glowing city below.

05

06

07

08

09

10

11

12

13

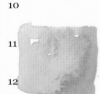

14

15

16

17

18

23 Friday Vendredi

01

02

03

04

05

06

07

08

09

10

11

12

13

14

15

16

17

Joyeux Noël

The post office was crazy today, as it is in the week before Christmas everywhere else in the world. Even though these packages won't arrive before Christmas, there is a relief by being able to truthfully say it's in the mail and it must be the fault of "*La Poste !*" which includes its own frustrated hand gestures.

It's true that *La Poste* delivers your packages whenever they feel up to it. It's also true that they feel superior to every other office in France. They even have their own museum.

La Poste was the first to give everyone a bank account, and many people still just use the bank at *La Poste* but I have no idea why when I see those lines and the trill of "*pas possibles*" coming from the cashiers. Still, even with their thin red lips, after not serving you well, they smile and wish you a hearty "*Joyeux Noël !*"

26 Monday Lundi   *Week 52*

01 You would think with all the feasting on the twenty-fifth that
    people would rest from the markets, but the twenty-sixth is the
02 beginning of preparing for the next big feast on New Year's Eve.
    The evening is a culinary showcase, featuring foie gras, oysters,
03 Champagne, an array of cheeses, and desserts. The French are
    thin but I have no idea how. France has banned plastic bags, so now
04 your tasty vittles come in charming paper bags.

05

06

07

08

09

10

11

12

13

14

15

16

17

18

27 Tuesday Mardi   *Week 52*

01 ## Lettering

02 Paris isn't for everyone. The waiters can be rude, the language can
be confusing, and I believe the administration to actually be mentally
03 ill. But Paris also gives every day. If you open your eyes, it will
reward you with gifts…sweet treats from every era. For me,
04 the greatest treasure is lettering.

05

06

07

08

09

10

11

12

13

14

15

16

17

18

ST.GASPARD DAY

01

02   The signage throughout Paris is spectacular. The curls of
beautifully set letters in soft, swirly fonts have me grabbing for my
03 camera all the time. The French don't have to make the letters
pretty but they do because they can and because they value beauty.
04 In fact, they are often offended by having to behold something that
isn't lovely to gaze upon. And I find that lovely.

05

06

07

08

09

10

11

12

13

14

15

16

17

18

29 Thursday Jeudi   *Week 52*

01 Then there are the surprise gifts, like snow in Paris. For all the

02 cold and all the rain, for some reason, having that cold and rain mix

03 to create snow doesn't happen very often. When it does, everyone goes outside to take in the familiar views now blanketed in white.

04   Snow is news in Paris. It's the main topic on everyone's lips, until of course, lunchtime. Then we are back to talking about food.

05

06

07

08

09

10

11

12

13

14

15

16   For half a day it snowed enough for an army of small snowmen

17 to appear. But then came the rain and all that remained were a few twigs and carrots.

18

01

03

04

05

06

07

08

09

10

For most people, there is a last night in Paris. But as Hemingway once said, "If you are lucky enough to have lived in Paris as a young man, then wherever you go for the rest of your life, it stays with you, for Paris is a moveable feast." After you unpack bags at home and close your eyes, Paris flutters behind the lids. Images of bustling boulevards, waiters pirouetting around tables, and glowing monuments appear. Or the memory of an accordion player comes along and his haunting melody lulls you to sleep.

11

12

13

14

15

Though you may leave Paris, Paris never really leaves you.

16

17

18

Thank you to my agent Laura Yorke of the Carol Mann Agency who is a master of getting it done. Thank you to BJ Berti, Courtney Littler, Felipe Cruz, and the rest of the team at St. Martin's Press for your guidance and attention to detail. Thank you to all my friends who patiently stood by as I stopped to take photos on the streets of Paris. And thank you to everyone who has subscribed to my Paris Letters. This nomadic artist is grateful for your support and enthusiasm. Finally, thank you to Krzysztof Lik who just nodded when I told him I was making a pretty book about Paris. He never has any doubt.

About the Author

Janice MacLeod is the original artist behind the Paris Letters project and author of the *New York Times* bestselling book, also called *Paris Letters*. She and her husband, the lovely Krzysztof Lik, travel to distant lands to sip coffee in front of breathtaking views.

Blog: *janicemacleod.com*
Shop: *etsy.com/shop/JaniceMacLeodStudio*